American Education
IN THE TWENTIETH CENTURY

The Library of Congress Series
in American Civilization
Edited by Ralph Henry Gabriel

American Education

IN THE TWENTIETH CENTURY

I. L. KANDEL

HARVARD UNIVERSITY PRESS

Cambridge, Massachusetts

1 9 5 7

Distributed in Great Britain by Oxford University Press· London

Library of Congress Catalog Card Number: 57–11658
Printed in the United States of America

PREFACE

A new period may be said to have opened with the beginning of the second half of the twentieth century. Whatever new problems arise in this period, a study of the developments of public-school education in the first half of the century is desirable if the concept of American education is to be understood and if the problems that have arisen and must still be solved are to be recognized. Lincoln once remarked that "if we would first know where we are and whither we are tending, we would then better judge what to do and how to do it." In that statement Lincoln put his finger on the value of the study of history.

The present book is limited to a presentation and discussion of public-school education — elementary and secondary education and the preparation of teachers. Private schools are discussed only to round out the picture of the education of all the children and youth of the nation. Higher education, that is, postsecondary school education, is to be dealt with in a separate volume in the series in which this book appears. For the same reason, since the book is one of a series that deals with different aspects of American civilization, the cultural forces that are reflected in education have not been dealt with in detail. That a new period is being inaugurated is clear from the convening of the President's Conference on Education in November 1955. Leaders of the second half of the century must, however, build on the tradition of American education to which so much was added in the first five decades.

I. L. KANDEL

ACKNOWLEDGMENTS

The author wishes to express his obligation to the following organizations and publishers for permission to quote from their publications: American Association of School Administrators; the Educational Policies Commission; Houghton Mifflin Company; National Council of State School Officers; *The New Republic*; and The Russell Sage Foundation. Full credit for the passages quoted is given in the relevant places in the References.

To Professor Ralph H. Gabriel, the editor of the series, American Civilization in the Twentieth Century, and to Dr. Waldo G. Leland, Director emeritus of the American Council of Learned Societies, the author is indebted for many helpful suggestions.

CONTENTS

CONTENTS

American Education

IN THE TWENTIETH CENTURY

CHAPTER I

American Education at Mid-Century

The second half of the twentieth century opens with a faith in education that not only is undiminished but rather is enhanced by the realization of the position of leadership achieved by the United States and of its responsibilities among the democracies of the world. This belief in the importance of education has been further strengthened by the recognition of the part that schools should play in preparing the future citizens of the country to meet their duties and responsibilities and to understand the complexities of modern life — economic, political, social, and cultural. Nevertheless, the state of education is one of greater confusion now than at any time in the history of the country.

While there are internal causes for this unrest, it also reflects the general uncertainty and confusion that have been developing during the last half century or more. The world is in a state of transition as a result of two devastating wars and of a widespread tendency to discard traditional values, forms, and conventions. This tendency has been no less marked in education than in other cultural activities like music, art, and literature in which experimentation and innovations have been characteristics of the first half of this century. To this uncertainty in the cultural field must be added the material changes produced by the progress of science and its applications in technology and means of communication which have not been without their influence in the field of educational theory and practice.[1]

The fifty years of this century have witnessed a radical transformation of a theory of education that has achieved notoriety both because of the vociferous claims put forward in its behalf and because the roseate picture was painted against a backdrop of an "evil" educational tradition. In general practice the schools underwent a certain improvement but this came more as a result of the contributions from child study and psychology than as a result of the new theories. Indeed, it has been a frequent cause of complaint by "Progressive" or "modern" theorists that the tradition of education and the teachers have been among the many obstacles to the general adoption of their ideas.[2]

In the first decades of the century, educators and the public were concerned primarily with the more general provision of schools, especially high schools, and with the raising of the standards for the preparation of teachers. On the professional side, interest was centered mainly on the improvement of methods of instruction and the content of the curriculum rather than on a transformation of the character and purpose of elementary and secondary education. The Herbartian philosophy of education was still dominant and was being perfected by its leading American exponents who had studied in Germany, Charles DeGarmo and Frank and Charles McMurray, and by the National Herbart Society for the Scientific Study of Education. But the challenge of a new philosophy of education and the new knowledge about interest, growth, and the learning process that came from child study and psychological research were already beginning to be considered.

With the gradual urbanization of the American people, the the public-school systems were on the eve of assuming the character of large-scale enterprises, and more was needed for their administration than a native capacity for management. At the same time, the study of education was gradually expanded from the study of methods of instruction and management for the preparation of classroom teachers, chiefly for elementary schools, to include preparation for an increasing number of special aspects in an expanding program of education.

The progress of this specialization is well exemplified by the emergence of a vast number of specialized organizations and associations for teachers of children at various stages of their education, for administrators and principals, and for parents and public. Alongside of this development there was an accumulation of research activities in teachers colleges and schools of education, in state and local bureaus of research, and in a variety of independent organizations. The contrast between the early years of this century and the present may be inferred from the differences in the functions of the teacher. At the beginning of the century the teacher was expected in the elementary school to impart a certain quantum of prescribed knowledge and information largely through a textbook, or in the secondary school to teach one or several allied subjects on which pupils would later be examined. The end of education was the harmonious development of the pupils. In the middle of the century the teacher was expected to be "a combination of psychiatrist, social scientist, scientist, and an individual of considerable culture who was also a man or woman of action" as well as a hygienist, guidance and welfare officer, and able to participate in extracurricular activities. The end of education is to develop "the whole personality" of the pupil and to prepare him to meet his "imperative needs" through an "education for life adjustment." [3]

The confusion referred to previously has resulted not only from the political, social, and economic conditions that followed the two World Wars, but also from the conflicts within the profession about the aims and methods of education itself and about the nature of values by which an individual should be guided and to which he should dedicate himself. On the material side, the most important factors that combine to render the immediate situation more difficult than could have been anticipated are the unexpected increase in the birth rate, the consequent pressing need for some years to come to provide more school buildings and more classrooms, the mobility of the population which has been caused not only by the shift of industry during and after World War II, but also by a desire to escape the overcrowding in the classes of urban schools, and the shortage of teachers who began during the war years to leave the profession for more remunerative employment in other careers. Because of the competition between different levels of governmental authorities in matters of taxation — federal, state, and local — the problem of the financial support of education has also become serious and has already led to the assumption of a greater share of the burden of educational expenditures by many state authorities. The gravity of the problem is strengthening the case for federal aid for education, the need for which began to be recognized by many educators nearly four decades ago, but whose enactment by Congress is always prevented by those who fear that federal aid would lead to federal control of education.[4]

More serious than these problems, however, are the uncertainty and confusion about the aims and methods of education, which since the end of World War II have reached the nature of a crisis. Conflicts about theories of education have been going on since World War I and were waged mainly by adherents of the traditional (or later "essentialist") point of view and the advocates of the "Progressive" (or later "modern") point of view. The late Professor Boyd H. Bode, writing in *The New Republic* in 1930, described the situation that still obtained in the middle of the century: "To the casual observer American education is a confusing and not altogether edifying spectacle. It is productive of endless fads and panaceas; it is pretentiously scientific and at the same time pathetically conventional; it is scornful of the past, yet painfully inarticulate when it speaks of the future. The tremendous activity now going on in education is evidence of farreaching social changes, but we do not seem to know what these changes signify or how they can be directed." In a later issue of the same journal, John Dewey stated that the reactions against traditional educational practices were marked by a great variety of new experiments but had no genuine sense of direction except an exaggerated and unfounded concept of freedom without a sense of responsibility or regard for the rights of others.[5]

Since the end of World War II the lay public has launched an avalanche of attacks on the public schools in all parts of the country. While many of the attacks were inspired by ulterior motives — unwarranted alarm at the rising cost of education, charges of responsibility for the rise in juvenile delinquency, the alleged fear of "Progressive" education as subversive, suspicion of indoctrination in favor of an international outlook or of a supergovernment, and so on — there were many well-intentioned and sincere citizens and professional educators who were critical of the trends in the theory and practice of education and who felt that the traditional values of the cultural heritage were being neglected. Others, again, felt that there had been a decline in the achievement of pupils in the fundamental subjects of reading, writing, and arithmetic. Unfortunately, the sincere and honest critics were not infrequently used by individuals and groups whose motives were not above suspicion.

The crisis in education, insofar as it concerns aims and methods, is the result of a certain feeling of discontent among that part of the public that is not apathetic about education. For some years now employers have complained that the product of the schools is not up to the standards that they expect in fundamentals. Parents are concerned about the progress of their children since marks have been abolished in favor of anecdotal reports, and about their preparation for college. High-school teachers complain that pupils come to them unable to read satisfactorily. A large percentage of the students who drop out of college before graduation give up their studies because of inadequate preparation, and a small number give up because they have already covered the work of the first two years of college in their high-school programs. At the same time there is widespread opinion to the effect that not enough attention is devoted to discovering and encouraging students of ability and promise.[6]

Paradoxically, while parents and employers, on the one hand, and high-school and college teachers on the other allege that students are not as well-grounded in their studies as they used to be and that standards have declined, research studies, employing objective tests, are cited to indicate not only that there has been no decline but in some places even an advance in achievement in the fundamentals. Both views may be correct, the tests being administered while the subjects are fresh in the minds of the pupils, and the other judgments being made some time after the subjects had been studied. No attempt seems to have been made to explain several questions: first, why many pupils have reached high school with only fourth-, fifth-, and sixth-grade competence in reading and arithmetic; second, why remedial classes in these subjects have to be established in high schools; and third, why a larger percentage of students than would be expected fails in college because of inability to read.

In defense of the system of public education, it may be said it has expanded so rapidly that the fact that the results are as good as they are is surprising. Before the outbreak of World War II the expansion had been so swift that opportunities for stocktaking and assessing results on a large scale did not present themselves.

From 1940 on, however, the facts about the amount of illiteracy in this country have been known; they were made available in the census of that year. Subsequently, some alarm was caused by the number of rejections by the armed services because of illiteracy, and by the number of young men of draft age who were admitted with such meager education that training had to be provided for them in the basic literacy skills. Still higher was the number of rejections based on physical and mental deficiency. To this may be added the shortage of candidates sufficiently well-prepared for admission to training courses for some of the specialized services.[7] But these defects which could be attributed to weaknesses in the educational system were speedily forgotten after the war.

The more professionalized the administration of education has become, the greater has been the tendency among its practitioners to become complacent and to resent criticism from any source. Such complacency and resentment may be common failings in all professions. Education, however, has not become so esoteric as to be beyond the capacity of laymen to understand it, despite the efforts among some educators to disguise meanings in a language of their own as an aspect and evidence of professional development and progress. Further, the administrator in order "to sell" education, tends to push the latest as the best, following the methods of the market place in an effort to prove alertness, initiative, and dynamic leadership often in the face of the silent opposition of the teachers who have to do the job.

Valuable as the development of a profession of education has been in both teaching and administration, it has been accompanied by a certain feeling of superiority to public opinion — which has not been overcome by the creation of parent-teacher organizations or by extensive publicity to enlist public interest. "Too many educators," it was stated in a recent yearbook of a professional organization, "have assumed that the purpose of public relations is 'to sell' the public their ideas.

They have ignored the attitudes, opinions, drives, and desires of the public itself." [8]

That the public and parents in general might have in mind the kind of education that they themselves enjoyed may indicate weakness or inability to recognize the need for change. But the sentiments of these laymen must be taken into account, and it is the failure on the part of the profession to give them due consideration that is one cause of the recent criticism of education. Theorists of education, who do not themselves have to stand before a class of children, have moved at a much faster rate than either the public or many members of the profession have been able to maintain. The Educational Advisory Committee and the Educational Advisory Council of the National Association of Manufacturers in *This We Believe About Education: A Statement Concerning Education in America* [9] wrote: "Schools are established and financially supported and teachers accept salaries and professional recognition to do a certain job. That is to give the next generation the best education that the current adult generation is able or willing to afford. However, what is meant by 'the best education,' and what duties are inherent in that term, are often the source of much controversy."

The conflicts in education are not confined to the public and the profession. They are found among educators themselves and are waged between "educators" and other members of the teaching profession, particularly in higher education. The conflict was well-illustrated by the acrimonious discussion of Professor Arthur E. Bestor's criticisms of the profession in *Educational Wastelands: The Retreat from Learning in Our Public Schools*. In 1952 Professor Bestor presented a series of resolutions to the Council of the American Historical Association. The 695 signatories to the resolutions represented most of the academic fields of study and expressed the belief "that the time has come for scholars and scientists to take a united stand in defense of sound intellectual

training in the public schools." Although the resolutions were
not then adopted, the Council authorized its president "to
appoint a committee to formulate and bring to the Association
a statement of its policy, to approach the other learned societies and professional educators on the subject of a common
position relative to the problem, and to discuss with them the
possible setting up of the proposed interdisciplinary educational commission." [10] A Committee on the Relation of
Learned Societies to American Education (CORLSAE) was
appointed in 1953 on the basis of a proposal by the secretaries
of the twenty-five constituent societies of the American
Council ol Learned Societies.

In contrast to the situation in other countries, there once
existed in the United States a certain unity among members
of the profession of teaching at all levels. Presidents of colleges and universities, superintendents of schools, and teachers used to sit in conference together. Before 1910 nationwide
committees on education included representatives of all levels
of educational institutions. This unity ended about 1910, and
the representatives of different levels of education drifted
apart. So many specialized organizations and societies have
sprung up, each claiming authority in its own field, that it is
impossible, except in the broadest terms, to arrive at a unified
view of the trends in American education. A Yearbook of the
American Association of School Administrators says: "Americans have a great dream of education for all and a tremendous
faith that the school works miracles. They believe firmly that
a good education guarantees an individual's success. What a
good education is and what sort of success they really want,
they seldom stop to analyze and no two people will give the
same answer." [11]

An earlier Yearbook of the same association makes a somewhat similar statement: "In reality, since the turn of the
century, the programs of the schools have been in flux. They
have not crystallized into commonly accepted functions and

purposes. Differences exist among them in quality, in character, in achievement, and in measures of support. While the
findings and hypotheses of objective psychology and the general acceptance of a pragmatic philosophy of education have
discredited much of formerly accepted practice, newer techniques have had slow acceptance. These, however, have been
considered so important by many educators that they have
become ends in themselves. It is, therefore, not surprising that
in this period of far reaching change a multiplicity of purposes in education have had their adherents and that controversies have been numerous. The result has been a spread
of objectives and a diffusion of teaching effort which has left
even the professional educator at a loss at times to explain
in its entirety just what the schools are attempting to do (and
which has given the ever ready critic of the schools some
basis for his cry 'the schools have failed')." [12]

The Harvard Committee in *General Education in a Free
Society* adds: "We are faced with a diversity of education
which, if it has many virtues, nevertheless works against the
good of society by helping to destroy the common ground
of training and outlook on which any society depends." [13]
The diversity is not the consequence of the existence of
private schools, but the result of experimentation guided at
one time by the interests of the pupils, at another by the
setting of the local community, and at still another by the
effort to adjust education to the rapidly changing conditions
of modern society. At present it would seem that the guiding
factors are to be found in the "needs" of children and adolescents who are to be trained to meet and resolve "the social
realities" and problems of the nation in this critical period.
Social engineering has in fact become the aim of some educational theorists, while others emphasize the development of
the unique personality of the individual.

Such uncertainty about the aims and purposes of education
is confusing not only to the public but also to the teachers

who have a responsibility both to their pupils and to the public. Some years ago a well-known educational publisher wrote an article under the revealing title "The Man Milliner in Education." [14] The process of changing fashions does not seem to have disappeared as may be confirmed by the following quotation from a book published nearly forty years later: "Many teachers are confused by the changes in theory and practice that appear to them to be advocated in rapid and bewildering sequence . . . Teachers are busy people in jobs that require the expenditure of much physical and nervous energy. They might keep up with many of the seemingly solid advances in educational science, if they were not further confused by theories that go beyond the facts, by disputes between experts on the level of theory. Not being trained in the scientific solution of educational problems, they often fail to realize that such differences of opinion are necessary if all aspects of scientific questions in education are to be in-dentified and explored. . . . They are intensely practical in adjusting what they do to the exigencies of the total 'situation' in which they find themselves." [15]

Many reasons may be adduced to explain this situation: first, the characteristic American tendency to venture into the untried and unexplored, to look for innovations, and to open up new frontiers; second, the attempt to apply to educa-tion the experimental methods which have contributed so much to the progress of science. Often, however, such at-tempts fail to take into account the fact that the scientist comes to his experimentation with a profound knowledge of and respect for the history and traditions of his subject. In the current mood of anti-intellectualism and irrationalism, with which they are charged some educational theorists prefer to rely on their own experience and to "create" their own values.

But the most pervasive and comprehensive reason for the frequent changes that are proposed is the fear of becoming "static," and a desire to be "dynamic" in theory and practice.

A dynamic theory is considered to be one that exhibits sensitivity to cultural and social and other changes, particularly the changes brought about by technology and applied science. The glamor of these changes has inspired faith in the employment of scientific method to solve everything. Schools are described as "the centre of vital currents of community life. They are touched by forces operating thoughout the nation . . . They must move along through time adding new ideas and discarding obsolete practices to keep in tune with the attitudes, beliefs, activities and hopes of the American people . . . Change and progress continue. Whether the future holds promise of better education through better schools depends upon the sensitivity of the classroom teachers and school administration to the trends surrounding us today. To fight change is futile; to drift with change is folly — we must rather seek to understand what is happening and with such powers as we possess try to use current developments as pathways to progress." [16]

A statement such as this leaves unanswered the question of how changes and progress have been produced in the development of American civilization and culture through the past generations despite an education which would today be described as "static" and insensitive to change. In the emphasis on dynamism and change two errors are inherent. The first is that all change means progress; a consequence of this notion is the prevalence of more interest in the idea of progress than in the progress of ideas. The second error arises from a failure to evaluate changes in terms of values or order of importance. In the main there has been a tendency to mistake the immediate surface currents for the permanent stream and, therefore, too much preoccupation with or fear of a "cultural lag." The severest condemnation of any theory or practice is to describe it as "obsolete" or "traditional." The strongest claim to consideration is to call the latest innovation "Progressive," or, since the idea of "Progressive" has become

suspected as subversive, to call it "modern." No sooner has
the movement for "education for the air age" been launched
that it is supplanted by a movement for "education for national defense," and that in turn "by education for the atomic
age." These changes took place in less than two decades.

This situation is not new, however; it was implicitly characterized in a statement by Santayana in *The Moral Background
of American Life* when he wrote: "Ideas are abandoned by
virtue of a mere change of feeling, without any evidence or
new arguments. We do not now refute our predecessors, we
pleasantly bid them good-bye. Even if all our principles were
unwittingly traditional, we do not like to bow openly to
authority."

These are some of the general causes of confusion and
uncertainty. They are also the causes of conflicts between
those who profess academic subjects and those who profess
"education." The former charge the latter with neglecting
subject matter and with emphasizing methods and pedagogical or professional subjects. The latter countercharge that the
former are bound by tradition and disregard the difficulties
of teaching children and adolescents. Some years ago Dr.
James Bryant Conant, then President of Harvard University,
in a lecture delivered at Teachers College, Columbia University, called for a truce between the two groups. The truce
has, however, never been arranged and the conflict continues.

On two points there is widespread agreement. The educational system must provide equality of opportunities to all
irrespective of race, color, creed, or economic status. The
main purpose of education is to transmit, preserve, and enrich the ideals of democracy. Both points express fundamental
ideals and both seem to be misinterpreted. Equality of educational opportunity is too often interpreted as identity of opportunity and any suggestion of providing different sections
for pupils of different intellectual abilities is dismissed as
undemocratic or as a return to the "aristocratic" selective

systems of other countries. One consequence of this position is that trend to mediocrity that Tocqueville had already described as a possible danger in the idea of equality. Another consequence is that a fluid curriculum has been developed at the postprimary or high-school level in which all the subjects are supposed to have equal value — a sort of democracy among subjects — or else it is proposed to displace them by "common learnings" or "life-adjustment education" adapted to the needs of all the pupils.

The concept of liberal education has either been discarded altogether, or else efforts have been made to describe vocational education as equally liberal as the traditional concept, or to insist that even the traditional concept was vocational since it was considered essential for further study and aedquate preparation for a professional career. But from whatever aspect the development of the past four decades is viewed, a decline in the understanding of educational values has taken place. Not only has there been a sacrifice of the notion of a liberal education, but even vocational education has proved to be unsatisfactory — for instance, when the needs of the Armed Forces and of industry had to be met on the outbreak of World War II.

Finally, still another consequence of the insistence upon identity of opportunity has been recognized only recently — the potential loss to the country as a whole through the neglect of able and talented youth, a recognition which led the Regents of the University of the State of New York to circulate a leaflet in 1954 under the title *Bright Kids: We Need Them.* In general, most of the difficulties of the high school arise from this attempt to make educational opportunities equal, while college-entrance examinations are regarded as a stumbling block to the reorganization of the high-school curriculum to meet the needs of all American youth. (See Chapter IV.)

Further, the interpretation of the ideal of democracy in

terms of school or classroom practice confuses authority with authoritarianism or autocracy. Starting from the premise that democracy is more than a form of government, that it is rather a way of life in which "each opinion is entitled to the same amount of respect as the next" and in which the wishes of the majority must prevail, there has been a tendency to encourage pupils to express their opinions out of their own experience without instilling into them the notion that opinions should be based on knowledge, information, and a sense of responsibility in expressing them. Too many classes conducted on this premise degenerate into debating societies in which the uninformed wishes of the majority must prevail and all must adjust themselves accordingly. Pupils, it is true, are urged to think but too often fail to put forward the effort to master the content with which they are to think. Nor, through fear of indoctrination, which has come to be regarded as an instrument of authoritarianism and propaganda and therefore undemocratic, may pupils be "told" anything; they must be free to find out for themselves, to be creative, and to exercise initiative and learn from their own experience. In other words, pupils must, according to this view, be taught how to think rather than what to think. They are expected to discover "the democratic way of life" by themselves without a map, and to arrive at their own values and standards — intellectual as well as moral — by trial and error; discipline was replaced by freedom but without its correlative of responsibility.

The drift of the times is suggested by another trend: the dominant note in preparing the younger generation to meet the domestic and world crises and to resolve its problems by emphasizing the "vital currents of the day" as though they will continue to wait for their solution until those now in school reach adulthood. But how these crises and problems have arisen and what their backgrounds are is left to be picked up incidentally as the need arises. In such a theory knowledge and information are not regarded as of the same importance as the acquisition of "the scientific method." In a world in which stress is placed on mutual understanding between nations and on international interdependence, the study of geography is neglected and the mastery of a foreign language is expected to result from exposure to two years of instruction. In science instruction, more attention is devoted to application of science in everyday life and to techniques than to the theory which is so essential as a basis for further study. Even the study of American history is too often "integrated" in or fused with a program of social studies.

The educational pendulum seems to swing from one extreme to the other. Because it is believed that in the past education dealt too much with what was remote from the pupils' immediate experience and needs, and because the values inherent in such instruction were considered to be "deferred," that is, to have meaning later in life, a swing has taken place to contemporaneity or modernism based on the immediate needs and experience of the pupils, and to functionalism or value for immediate use.

Another example of the change in educational theory and practice which paralleled the surrender of traditional values was the relaxation of discipline in the school and classroom. On the plea that in the past discipline was rigid and authoritarian and made for docile obedience, "external" discipline, as it was called, was abandoned in favor of freedom in the expectation that pupils would in this way learn to discipline themselves, to grow into self-disciplined individuals. Events proved the fallacy of such a theory which, when put into practice and as a result of many other factors arising out of social changes, resulted at the end of the first half of the century in a serious outbreak of juvenile delinquency for which the school was not alone responsible, although the allegation of such responsibility was not infrequently made.

This change in the theory of discipline was accompanied

by another swing of the pendulum in both curriculum and methods of instruction. That swing was from what the critics of the past have called "passive learning" to "activity methods." Passive learning, it was charged, was authoritarian in character, and placed the emphasis on indoctrination, drill, repetition, and rigorous discipline. Through activity methods it was expected that pupils would learn better from their own experience with an activity curriculum based on their own interests instead of by rote material which represented adult and remote interests. Activity methods and the study of materials of immediate interest to the pupils would, it was claimed, challenge them, encourage self-expression, and develop personality. This was the theory that dominated elementary education for many years, and had some advocates in secondary education.

In high schools, the theory manifested itself in a shift from emphasis on the development of intelligence to emphasis on the equal importance of a cultivation of emotions and attitudes in the development of character and personality. This was more acceptable because of the rapidly increasing enrollment of boys and girls for whom neither the traditional academic curriculum nor the vast array of new courses that were accumulated in the half century was apparently suited. The increasing number of "maladjustments," intellectual and emotional, and the problem of adapting the curriculum to individual differences of ability and interest led to the establishment of systems of guidance and counseling but did not solve the confusion in the education of the adolescent.

As will appear later, the changes in curriculum and methods, in theory at any rate, were based on attempts to find short cuts to an understanding of the problems of contemporary citizenship without providing an adequate foundation in any of the necessary disciplines. Global and integrated courses took the place of the separate subjects which might be studied incidentally as they were needed. The change in the aims of elementary and secondary education at the end of the nineteenth century to those of postwar education was posed in the previously cited *Schools for a New World.* "Can America build a school system that is able to explain the fundamental issues of these postwar years to the people? Can these schools stimulate the social action necessary to the successful resolving of America's problems? " Such were the tasks outlined for the schools in the Twenty-fifth Yearbook of the American Association of School Administrators, published in 1947, although it was already known that some 60 per cent of the pupils in high schools derived no benefit from their stay and that many pupils in high schools had only fourth-, fifth-, or sixth-grade reading ability.

Not until the challenge of the "cold war" and the subsequent challenge of the USSR in trained scientific manpower did the urgency of two problems, which are facets of the same problem, begin to be widely realized. Of these, the first was the need of discovering and educating pupils of talent and ability, and the second, the inadequate supply of trained ability in the sciences — especially physics and chemistry — and engineering. The inadequate preparation and the shortages had been known by those who had watched the gradual changes that were taking place in the high schools and were disturbed by the decline in the status of academic subjects — as much in the humanities and social sciences as in the natural sciences to which most of the publicity came to be directed.

The confusion of the postwar period was further increased by the realization that there was a growing shortage of teachers, of schools, and of classrooms, and that inadequate efforts were being made to meet the situation. These shortages due in part to the unpopularity of teaching as a career and in part to the rapidly increasing enrollments, are, of course, responsible for the larger classes which are becoming marked everywhere in American cities. The effort to escape from this condition either by sending children to private schools or by moving to suburbs has resulted in the same conditions being produced as rapidly there as in the cities. For the present there seems to be no solution in sight; opponents of federal aid assert that the states can find the money to meet the shortages by revising methods of taxation. The case for federal aid, however, is more cogent than it has ever been since the time when such aid was proposed nearly four decades ago. Until a formula has been discovered that will guarantee freedom from federal control, it is not likely that such aid will be forthcoming. In the meantime, many children are being deprived of their opportunities for education or are attending schools under extremely adverse conditions — crowded classrooms and substandard teachers.

Despite these deficiencies, which are becoming increasingly clear the main strengths of American education have not been undermined. American education continues to be rooted in a deep faith in its importance and value for a democratic society. Citizens throughout the country recognize that only through education can freedom be guaranteed and preserved. Unlike the schools in most other countries, the American school is not used as an instrument to propagate the policy of government or to preserve the privileges of a social class. The schools are in a real sense the people's schools. Almost a century ago the public school was defined by the Secretary of the Massachusetts Board of Education as "a school established by the public, supported chiefly or entirely by the public, controlled by the public, and accessible to the public upon terms of equality, without special charge for tuition." Public education is necessarily dependent, therefore, upon public opinion and support — moral and financial, a fact that has been illustrated in the last decade and clearly recognized earlier in the extensive publicity given to education.

The external accomplishments illustrate the profound faith in education. The most striking buildings in most communities are the school edifices that would be ornaments in many a metropolis abroad. The finest example of American idealism is the provision of equality of educational opportunities which has made elementary education nearly universal everywhere in the country and high-school education available for 75 per cent of the nation's youth between fourteen and seventeen years of age. The provision of education has again been recognized as "an investment in people" as it was formerly stated by Horace Mann. Nevertheless, a sound system of education cannot be built on uncertain and unstable aims. The inventiveness which has dominated educational fashions for so long could well be turned to discovering ways of improving the recruitment, preparation, and status of the teachers in ways commensurate with the important function that they must perform in preserving and strengthening a democratic society. In the end, the community as well as the professional educators must share in what solutions are achieved for such vital and pressing problems as those arising within the field of education.

CHAPTER 11

The Public and Its Schools

In a very real sense the American schools belong to the public. They are the schools of the people rather than of governments as in most other countries. It is the public that determines their character and, although executive functions have been placed increasingly in the hands of expert officials, it is ultimately the desires and opinions of the public that prevail in the conduct and administration, and even the instructions in the school systems. In 1859 George Boutwell, Secretary of the Massachusetts Board of Education, defined the public school as "a school established by the public — supported chiefly or entirely by the public, controlled by the public, and accessible to the public on terms of equality, without special charge for tuition." The definition conveys only in part the significant role which the public has come to play in the provision, maintenance, and control of the nation's schools.

THE DEVELOPMENT OF PUBLIC INTEREST

The first fifty years of the present century witnessed a gradual expansion of the interest taken by the public in all that concerns education. The expansion of scope and opportunities in education would not have been possible without the coöperation of the public. Nor does it detract from the interest shown that criticisms of the schools have been ex-

pressed from time to time during the half century — at one
time against the increased cost, at another, against the narrow
or else the extensive curriculum, and at still another, against
the unsatisfactory standards of achievements both scholastically and morally. Instead of being deplored or considered
inimical to the schools, criticism should be welcomed as a
spur to constant re-examination and scrutiny. Criticisms may
be regarded as evidence of a certain attitude of alertness on
the part of the public, and without them control of education
(as of other public affairs) would fall into the hands of a
bureaucracy. The American system of education in the
middle of the twentieth century is the result of the varied
competing influence of pressure groups. Such groups may
be distinguished according to the interests they endeavor to
promote — whether for the general welfare or for narrow,
selfish ends. The representatives of the public in boards of
education and their administrative officials have frequently
been called upon to distinguish between the two forms of
pressure, one to advance the special interests of a group —
political, religious, economic, or commercial — and the other
to participate in building a new social order and promoting
social reform. Many subjects added to the curriculum of both
the elementary and the secondary schools and decried as fads
and frills were introduced in response to public demand.
Such subjects include, among others, music, art, crafts, practical and industrial arts.

Historically, public interest in education was developed
in the district system. There the responsibility for providing,
maintaining, and administering a school devolved on the local
residents and taxpayers to whom the school-board members
were in turn accountable. Local interest was rooted in that
faith in education expressed by the nation's leaders from the
time of Washington to the present. Not until the end of the
nineteenth century when more than the local school was required to meet the nation's needs for well-educated citizens

was this interest challenged and redirected to the support of larger areas of educational administration. The persistence of local loyalties has been manifested in the movement to combine districts in order to make possible better schools and to provide equality of educational opportunities to all boys and girls. The movement developed slowly at first and gained momentum after World War I and resulted in a considerable reduction in the number of school districts and the establishment of consolidated schools.

Referring to education at the end of the nineteenth century (1896), James Bryce wrote as follows: "It has hitherto been not only a more distinctively local matter, but one relatively more important than in most parts of Europe. And there is usually a special administrative body, often a special administrative area, created for its purposes — the school committee and the school district. The vast sum expended on public instruction has already been mentioned. Though dealt with primarily by the smallest local circumscription, there is a growing tendency for both the county and the state to interest themselves in the work of instruction by way of inspection and to some extent pecuniary subventions. Not only does the county often appoint a county superintendent, but there are in some states county high schools and (in most) county boards of education, besides a state board of commissioners." [1]

The district system, however, was inadequate to meet the new problems that mounted in number and variety in the twentieth century. The rapid development of industry and the progress of mass production were accompanied by a change in the distribution of the country's population. Americans were still a predominantly rural people in 1900. The division was 60.3 per cent rural and 39.7 per cent urban. By 1950 the distribution was more than reversed; 64 per cent of the population was urban and 36 per cent rural, and of the rural population less than 50 per cent were technically farm people. During the same period, the population had increased from 75,994,575 to 150,697,361.

The consequences of industrial development and of urbanization were crucial for education. The increased wealth of the nation as a whole and of the cities in particular made it possible to introduce an expanded school system based not only on the traditional faith in education, but also on the ideal of equality of opportunity for every boy and girl. The increase in family income enabled parents to keep their children in school longer provided courses suited to their abilities and interests were offered — a condition which was to manifest itself a few years later in the new century.

EXTENSION OF COMPULSORY ATTENDANCE LAWS

These conditions enabled school authorities to enforce compulsory attendance laws more effectively. At the beginning of the century thirty-two states and the District of Columbia had already placed such laws on their statute books; between 1900 and 1910 the list was increased by the addition of ten more states; and in 1918 Mississippi became the last state to round out the list and enact a compulsory attendance law, though it was not at first mandatory for the whole state. The developments since the end of World War I, which reflected the economic conditions of the country, showed the gradual decline of satisfactory employment opportunities for adolescent boys and girls as well as changes in the educational programs available in order to keep them in school. Although the ages for the beginning and the end of the compulsory attendance period varied from state to state, the trend was to raise the age for leaving school, as is shown in the following summary based on a report of the U.S. Office of Education issued in 1950.[2]

In thirty-two states, attendance was required between the ages of seven and sixteen: Alabama, Arkansas, Connecticut, Delaware, Florida, Georgia, Idaho, Illinois, Indiana, Iowa,

Kansas, Kentucky, Louisiana, Maryland, Massachusetts, Mississippi, Missouri, Nebraska, New Jersey, New York, North Carolina, Oregon, Rhode Island, South Carolina, South Dakota, Tennessee, Texas, Vermont, Virginia, West Virginia, Wisconsin, and Wyoming.

Seven states required attendance between the ages of eight and sixteen: Arizona, California, Colorado, Minnesota, Montana, New Hampshire, Washington.

Two states, Maine and North Dakota, required attendance between the ages of seven and seventeen. In two states, Nevada and Olkahoma, the ages of attendance were seven and eighteen. In the remaining five states the age varied: Michigan, six to sixteen; New Mexico, six to seventeen; Ohio, six to eighteen; Pennsylvania, eight to seventeen; and Utah, eight to eighteen.

The customary age at which children enter school, however, is six, and in all the compulsory attendance laws provision is made for pupils to obtain "work permits" on completing a certain grade before reaching the prescribed leaving age.

The same circumstances that stimulated the development of effective compulsory attendance laws were also conducive to a gradual extension of the school year which was extended from an average of 144.6 days in 1900 to an average of 178 days in 1949–50. In the rural areas school attendance improved gradually with the improvement of roads and means of transportation, and later the consolidation of schools facilitated by these means of communication. The growing humanitarianism and recognition of the social consequences of better relations between employers and labor were also reflected in a new attitude to children and to education. As will be pointed out later in detail, a new era began at the turn of the century in the attitude toward the child and new theories of education entered into competition with each other to improve the lot of children at home and in school.

The United States, more definitely than any other country, inaugurated in 1900 what Ellen Key called *The Century of the Child*, an era that was to manifest both good and bad practices educationally.

Education for citizenship and the Americanization of the immigrant, both young and old, were considered to be primary aims of school. As late as 1919, a distinguished educator was still able to write that "a pressing need today is that our national government shall undertake a national campaign to eliminate some of our national weaknesses and dangers. We must resolutely set to work, during the respite from the immigrant flood which the World War promises for a time to give us, to Americanize the foreign-born in our midst. We must abolish illiteracy, and make English our one language." [3] Eventually, however, Americanization ceased to be a serious problem in education, except in the preparation of adult immigrants who were planning to become naturalized.

Preparation for citizenship became and remained a major preoccupation of both elementary and secondary schools when they were challenged by alien ideologies after World War I, by the fear of loss of morale during the depression and in the years immediately preceding and following World War II. With the turn of the century there began to take place not only a shift of emphasis from the subject to the child, but a more specific emphasis on the preparation of the individual to be an intelligent citizen and a trained worker. Such changes were reflections of the increasing complexity of life that resulted from the enlarging industrial development, the rising standards of living, the new sense of nationalism and national destiny that followed the Spanish-American War, the rapid succession of new inventions and the availability of the automobile, the gradual development of cultural independence and the place assumed by the fine arts and

music, and the increase of publications — all these developments changed the character of American life and challenged
thinking. The new media of communication — the telephone,
the radio, television, the motion pictures and other devices
for audio-visual instruction — while they have not fulfilled
the best that was expected of them, did provide a wide array
of vicarious experiences which helped to break down localism
and to provide common areas of interaction.

At the same time, the scope of education had to be extended.
Elementary education and the simple curriculum of the nineteenth century, it was argued, did not provide an adequate
preparation for life in the twentieth century, and even the
solid achievements of the educational tradition were decried.
The secondary-school curriculum was open to the criticisms
not only that it was no longer adequate for the new culture,
but that it was not suited to the abilities or needs of the youth
who were flocking to the high schools in increasing numbers.
Both elementary and secondary education were attacked
early in the century because they were not functional and
dynamic. Not infrequently changes were advocated because
change was equated with progress, a confusion to which the
American public was susceptible.

There were sound reasons for changes in elementary and
secondary education, nevertheless, which were contributed
by the new centers for the study of education that began to
be established around 1900. The faculty psychology had already been under attack both in Germany and in the United
States during the last decade of the nineteenth century. Its
correlates, the idea of formal discipline and transfer of training, were subjected to critical investigation by American psychologists in the early years of the present century and, if
not disproved as was frequently claimed, were hedged by a
number of reservations. On the psychological and philosophical sides, new concepts of interest and new theories of
the learning process began to affect the development and

practices of both elementary and secondary education. To these developments the child-study movement, which had already been initiated in 1888, made important contributions, while the educational philosophy of John Dewey introduced a new note on the relations of school and society and linked up the philosophy with the new child psychology and the interests of the child. For nearly two decades the influence of these new developments was found principally in private experimental schools, out of which in 1919 came the Progressive Education Association. The so-called progressive ideas did not find their place in public schools which were dominated, on the one side, by the nineteenth-century practice of the "recitation" method, and on the other, by the American modifications of the theory of the German philosopher, Johann Friedrich Herbart.

The economic and cultural changes, the development of larger urban centers, and advances in the study of education from the psychological and philosophical aspects all pointed to the greater social and national significance of the schools. Compulsory education was extended; the curricula and methods of instruction in the elementary schools began to be adapted to the new demands that reflected a changing culture; the high schools had to turn their attention to meeting the needs of constantly increasing enrollments and to providing curricula suited to individual differences in ability, interests, and occupational plans of the pupils; and, finally, the changing situation required the adoption of higher standards for the preparation of teachers. Not only did changes begin to take place in the curricula and methods of the schools, but a movement to reorganize the educational system, already proposed in the last decade of the nineteenth century, began to take form; six years of primary and six years of secondary education, divided into three years of junior and three years of senior high school, began before the end of the first decade of the present century to displace the traditional eight years of elementary and four years of secondary education in many school systems. Further, to meet the varied economic and individual needs of pupils, different types of high schools — manual, technical, and household-arts schools — began to be established in the early years of the century, only to be amalgamated into the "comprehensive" high school catering to boys and girls of all ranges of abilities and interests. The comprehensive and coeducational high school became the characteristically American form of secondary education with curricular and other problems which, as will appear in a later chapter, have not yet been settled.

EDUCATION, A MAJOR PUBLIC ENTERPRISE: ITS ADMINISTRATION

Education thus became one of the major public enterprises of the country. The enrollments in public elementary and high schools rose from 15,503,110 in 1899–1900 to 25,709,524 in 1949–50. The enrollment of pupils in high schools had risen from 519,000 in 1899–1900 to 5,707,000 in 1949–50. The current expenditures on education rose from $214,965,000 in 1899–1900 to $5,837,643,000 in 1949–50. The cost per pupil in average attendance rose from $20.21 in 1899–1900 to $258.-85 in 1949–50.[4] The expenditures in 1899–1900 represented 1.20 per cent of the national income, while those for 1949–50 were about 2 per cent of the national income. In the 50 years that elapsed, the number of administrative units decreased from about 150,000 to 83,237, the larger areas of administration providing a larger taxing area and consequently a better opportunity to implement the ideal of equality of educational opportunities.

An expansion on the scale described called for officials or administrators who were familiar with the educational problems on both the administrative and the instructional side. As the educational systems developed in size and scope of activities the administrative staff grew in numbers and in variety

of specialization. The most important function of the administrator or superintendent of schools is to exercise leadership
and to bring his influence to bear on both the public and the
instructional staff. "Leadership has been defined as the ability
to generate enthusiasm for a project and to inspire work
toward its solution. . . . Leadership also consists of getting
people to think through a project and arrive at a group decision — not to accept the ideas of the leader without question." [5] This is a further confirmation of the American principle that the schools belong to the public and progress depends
upon winning the support and confidence of the public. The
goodwill of the public must be secured by keeping it informed and educating it to understand what the schools are
doing or planning to do. At the same time it has become
incumbent on the administrator to know the public whom he
is appointed to serve.

In contrast to most other countries, where the administration of education is generally bureaucratic in character, the
American public, if not directly, then through a great variety
of voluntary groups and through its school boards or boards
of education maintains an active interest in its schools. Among
the earliest of such groups were the Child Study Association,
whose history goes back to 1888, and the National Congress
of Parents and Teachers, which began its existence in 1897
as the National Congress of Mothers; both organizations have
published journals which have had a considerable influence.
Parent-Teacher Associations have been established throughout the country. The service clubs (Rotary, Kiwanis, and
Lions) and women's clubs have always taken an interest in
education; the leading labor unions have their education
committees, and on the management side the National Association of Manufacturers and the United States Chamber of
Commerce have through committees shown an active interest
in education. A watchful eye is kept on the schools by such
patriotic organizations as the Daughters of the American

Revolution, the Veterans of Foreign Wars, and the American Legion.

As the schools began to be subjected to increasing criticism — during the depression years and after World War II — the importance of establishing continuous public relations was recognized as paramount. Thus, the Educational Policies Commission, published a statement in 1938 saying that "if the schools are to serve democracy, they must be kept in close touch with the people locally. Whatever the general program that may be mandated by the state, the schools will fail of their purpose unless they reflect the interests, the ideals, and the devotion of the community which they serve. It is reasonable to suppose that local school systems be adjusted to the peculiar needs of the local area. It is essential that the professional staff of the school system be supported in its work by the participation of intelligent citizens in the development of the curriculum and in the provision of experiences outside of the school for the children enrolled. In order that the schools may most certainly represent the people, it is most important that the people choose their representatives for places on the board of education without reference to party politics. It is essential that those so chosen keep closely in contact with the public which they serve and with the professional staff which they employ. Only on the basis of complete and wholehearted coöperation among the professional staff of the school system, members of the board of education, and the community at large, can education effectively serve democracy." [6]

The National Council of Chief State School Officers in a pamphlet, *Our System of Education,* issued in 1950, made a somewhat similar statement on the basic principle of American educational administration: "Local school boards and other state education authorities represent the public in the administration of education. Working with their professional staffs, these authorities are responsible for carefully planned programs of education and for obtaining the participation of the people in planning the kinds of schools and the education they need and want.

"Local and state education authorities should strive constantly to make available information needed by citizens to participate intelligently in the planning and conduct of the public schools. All available means of communication should be used to challenge their interest and to promote the widest possible participation in formulating programs of public education. Local and state education authorities should provide functioning research services to supply the facts needed for complete understanding of the program of the schools and all members of the staff should share in the development of this understanding." [7]

Toward the end of the half century, teachers were expected to make contacts with the homes and parents of their pupils and with their communities, partly to establish confidence and intelligent understanding of education among the public, and partly to familiarize themselves with the cultural and other backgrounds of their pupils and of the community in order to adapt the work of the school to both.

EDUCATION AND PUBLIC RELATIONS

After World War II three circumstances combined to intensify the importance of securing the support and confidence of an alert public. These were the mounting criticisms of, if not direct attacks on, the public schools, a realization that the enrollments in the schools would increase as a result of the high postwar birth rate involving increased expenditures for new schools and classrooms as well as for more teachers and higher salaries, and a recognition that the challenge of alien ideologies must be met by more intense and more pervasive emphasis on promoting intelligent understanding of the meaning of democracy and the democratic way of life. The movement to enlist the support and interest of the public more actively may also have been influenced by fear of the trend to centralization manifested during the depression and the War, and the possible removal of control from the local communities.

In May 1949, with financial support from the Carnegie Corporation, The Fund for the Advancement of Education, The Fund for the Republic, the General Education Board, the Rockefeller Brothers Fund, the Alfred P. Sloan Fund, and the New York Community Trust, the formation of the National Citizens Commission for the Public Schools was announced. This commission, established as a nonprofit corporation for the improvement of the public schools, consists of citizens not professionally identified with education, religion, or politics. Its purpose is to promote the establishment of state-wide and local committees to serve as advisory bodies to the education authorities and to promote public interest in education and its policies, and in legislation dealing with the schools.

The commission has published a number of pamphlets and study guides on various aspects of education that are of public concern for laymen and for the guidance of local committees. Its basic principles are in line with the statements on the importance of public participation in educational affairs that have already been cited. The commission's statement is as follows: "The problem of its children's schools lies at the heart of a free society. None of man's public institutions has a deeper effect upon his conduct as a citizen, whether of the community, of the nation, or of the world. The goal of our public schools should be to make the best in education available to every American child on completely equal terms. Public school education should be constantly reappraised and kept responsive both to our educational traditions and to the changing times.

"With these basic beliefs in mind, the National Commission for the Public Schools has set for itself two immediate goals:

To help Americans realize how important our public schools are to our expanding democracy; To arouse in each community the intelligence and will to improve our public schools." Citizens in every community were urged to hold meetings to familiarize themselves with the problems and practices of education and to dedicate the total citizens' resources to their improvement.

This is the note on which the second half century of education was to develop — strong emphasis on the coöperation of all who have an interest in education — parents, the public, voluntary groups, professional associations, and professional staffs. It is from all these groups rather than from governments that leadership in education has come in the United States. That leadership has been exercised in a variety of ways.

One of the most important functions of the school administrators, as already mentioned, is to keep the public informed about the work of the schools in their area and to "sell" education. This information is disseminated by the publication of bulletins, the distribution of newsletters, publicity in the local papers, and particularly in the new form of the annual reports. At the beginning of the century the education reports were badly printed, formidable documents, mainly statistical and issued with no apparent expectation of being read. In the past quarter of a century they have been replaced in a number of areas by beautifully printed and illustrated booklets that are clear and informative, even though at times they play up the best and conceal the less pleasing aspects of the systems with which they deal. Parent-teacher meetings are more frequently organized. Once a year, usually in November, an American Education Week is proclaimed under the sponsorship of the National Education Association, the American Legion, and the United States Office of Education, and devoted to a special theme with public lectures and visits to the schools. Close relations have been established between the school systems and their local presses and education has become newsworthy. Educational journalism has been developed as a special field, the number of writers employed by some of the nation's leading newspapers and devoting their time to the more than seven hundred educational journals was sufficient to warrant the formation in 1946 of the Educational Writers Association. That the methods of reaching the public are many and varied is in itself significant that still more needs to be done to arouse the public from a certain apathy and inertia was indicated by the establishment of the National Citizens Commission for the Public Schools.

The teachers colleges and schools of education, still in their infancy when the century opened, have been important centers not only for the preparation of teachers and administrators but also for advancing the study of education and for research. Many local and state authorities established their own research bureaus, whose directors in 1915 formed themselves into the National Association of Directors of Educational Research which in 1922 became the American Educational Research Association. The National Society for the Study of Education established in 1892 as the National Herbart Society, the National Society of College Teachers of Education, and a large number of societies and associations were created to promote the study of special aspects of education (administration, supervision, curriculum, secondary education, social studies), many becoming affiliates of the National Education Association. This organization with more than 600,000 members, established in 1857, has gained in status, influence and prestige in the last thirty years of the first half of the present century. It has served as a center for ventilating the problems of education; it has sought through one of its committees to safeguard the freedom of teachers; it has itself maintained a Research Division since 1922. From the point of view of public relations the most significant organization is the Educational Policies Commission established in 1936 under the sponsorship of the National Education Association and the American Association of School Administrators. The purposes of the Commission were "to stimulate thoughtful, realistic, long-term planning with the teaching profession; to encourage desirable changes in educational purposes, procedures, and organization; to review recommendations for the improvement of education; to make the best practices in education known and used throughout the country; and to develop more effective coöperation among various groups interested in educational improvement." Among its many publications the most valuable were the earliest which dealt with fundamental problems of the relations of education and American democracy.

While the National Education Association with its member organizations covers the whole field of education, the American Council on Education, created in 1918, devoted itself primarily to problems of higher education, but was associated with the work of the American Youth Commission, organized in 1925 with Newton D. Baker as chairman and Owen D. Young as vice-chairman, and with the inquiry into teacher education (1937–45). The activities of both the A.C.E. and the A.Y.C. have played an important part in the progress of American education.

EDUCATIONAL SURVEYS

Among the best examples that illustrate the dependence of education on public confidence and support has been the development of surveys or investigations to assess or evaluate school systems or to suggest the improvements that need to be made. In the absence of a central government agency that could exercise its authority and control over local administrative units, there developed the practice of inviting experts in education to investigate school systems, either because there were signs of public dissatisfaction or because outside opinion was desirable to assess the work of school system in comparison with that of other systems or in the light of sound theory.

The survey method first employed in Boise, Idaho, in 1910, spread rapidly throughout the country, and experts and their staffs were invited to survey city and state systems. The experts were generally expected to make recommendations for improvement on the basis of their investigations. Investigations might cover every aspect of a school system or deal only with some special aspects, such as administration, records and accounts, elementary or secondary education, the curriculum, buildings and business management, and finance. At first the results of the survey were based mainly on the judgment of the investigator. But it was not long before the new methods of testing mental ability and of objective measurement of achievements began to be used extensively as they were developed in the centers for the study of education. The benefits were mutual — the research instruments were tested in practical situations and the results enriched at least that branch of education which could be denominated as scientific.

The leading educators of the day conducted such surveys: Leonard P. Ayres of the Russell Sage Foundation; E. E. Brown, the U. S. Commissioner of Education; Ellwood P. Cubberley of Stanford University; E. C. Elliott of the University of Wisconsin; Abraham Flexner of the General Education Board; Paul H. Hanus of Harvard University; Charles H. Judd of the University of Chicago; and George D. Strayer of Teachers College, Columbia University. A number of philanthropic foundations — the Carnegie Foundation for the Advancement of Teaching, the General Education Board, the Rockefeller Foundation, and the Russell Sage Foundation — were also associated, either directly or financially, with the survey movement. After World War I a number of nationwide studies, also financed by foundations, were conducted on the place of the classics, modern languages, and mathematics in the curriculum of the high schools. The United States Bureau, later Office, of Education also conducted school surveys on invitation and on a nationwide scale investigated the status of secondary education (1932) and the education of teachers (1933) in the country.

The success of the surveys lay mainly in the conviction which the results aroused. It was a common practice to present these results to the public at meetings held before the results were published and to provide an opportunity for discussion. As in the case of all other methods of public relations in education, the meetings and the publications were intended to be educational methods to develop understanding of the problems involved and the improvements recommended.

The surveys had one other beneficial result. The majority of the experts were themselves professors of education. They were in a position to broaden the training of their students, whom they associated with themselves as staff members, on the practical side of their work. The literature of education was enriched and served as another method of developing national and comparative standards. Most important of all, since the surveys were undertaken at the request of the public out of concern for the welfare and progress of its own education system, authority and control were not surrendered to an external agency and whatever progress was to be made, following a survey, was left entirely to the public.

The importance of this principle was clearly emphasized in an affirmation by the Educational Policies Commission. "Centralization in the control, administration, and financing of education," said the Commission in 1938, "is very apt to lead to a mediocre school system and a lack of progressive development of the program of public education. With well-developed local units for school administration it is certain that some communities will develop leadership which will be effective in improving education. It is in these areas, in which experimentation occurs and in which idealism leads people to make sacrifices in order to maintain an adequate system of education, that demonstrations will be made which may later affect the whole programs of education throughout a state or even throughout the nation. Most of the great reforms in education have originated in the schools of some local community; they were not decreed by a central authority." [8]

THE STATES AND EDUCATION

American educators are determined to safeguard their independence against a tendency by the states in the last three decades to assume a larger share of the cost of education. Fear lest control be removed still further has prevented the adoption of the many proposals to provide federal aid. In the first half of the century there has been a considerable change in the sources of revenues for the maintenance of school systems. In 1899–90 local taxation provided 70 per cent, the state appropriations 17 per cent, and permanent funds and other sources 13 per cent of the revenues. Fifty years later local taxes provided for a little over half of the revenues, 51.2 per cent; 6.1 per cent came from counties, 39.8 per cent from the states, and 2.9 per cent from the Federal Government.

The change was brought about by several causes. The Federal Government, since the beginning of the century, has entered into competition with local and state authorities in the field of taxation. The cost of adequate systems of education has increased beyond the financial capacity of local authorities to provide for. Finally, the character of the state education authorities has changed and the states have assumed a more important position in the administration of education and in the determination of policies. The responsibility of the states has increased because they have been assigned the function of administering funds granted by the federal government for various services including vocational education, school lunches, the Civilian Conservation Corps and National Youth Administration in the depression years, and defense training and other activities during World War II.

Since the Constitution is silent on the subject, education is a function of the state, in fact. By the Tenth Amendment it was left to the several states as a power not prohibited to them nor delegated to the United States government. The functions of state departments of education have expanded since 1900 when they were responsible only for seeing that the state education laws were executed and for collecting statistical information. At the present time both their responsibilities and the prestige have increased. Before World War I a distinguished educator in referring to the differences in the provision of education between the states and within each state could describe the position of the state authorities as follows: "It is in the attempt to eliminate these differences and to unify the school system of any state that the need of a constructive educational policy is evident. In some states this seems to be almost lacking on the part of the state's educational authorities, and, so far as it exists at all it is developed and carried forward rather by the leading teachers of the state. The political nature of the chief educational office and the constant rotation in that office almost preclude the possibility of a continuous educational policy. In but a few states do we find evidences of any well thought-out educational policy, carried out over any period of time." [9]

By 1950 the character of the state administration had changed. This was both because of the increased recognition given to the importance of expanding educational opportunities and because of the higher caliber of the members of state boards and chief state-school officers engaged in the administration of education, even though in most states the method of appointment continued to be by popular election. The function of the state in relation to education has been described simply in the following statements by the National Council of Chief State School Officers: "The State is sovereign with respect to its basic responsibility for establishing and administering a program of education adapted to the needs of its citizens and for the necessary coördination of all education activities within its borders. The State is responsible for determining the extent and quality of educational services to be provided by its foundation program of education and for assisting local boards of education to assume their responsibility in providing and additional services." [10]

Accordingly, the state establishes minimum standards of education and has the power to enforce them; it provides an increasing share of the funds for the support of education; it formulates policies and evaluates their development; it promotes the maintenance of school records and reports not only for purposes of information but also for comparisons; it serves in an advisory and consultative capacity; it is responsible for administering and distributing funds appropriated for educational services by the federal government. These functions fall within the scope of general control and supervision, but beyond these it has taken over the training in large part and the certification of teachers and prescribing minimum salary schedules; it defines the courses of study and many maintain lists of accredited institutions which may or may not overlap other lists maintained by regional or national accrediting agencies.

State departments of education consist normally of the board of education and the chief state-school officer, a title which is replacing the earlier "superintendent of public instruction," and their staffs. In most states the members of the state board are appointed by the Governor or are ex officio members. The chief state-school officers, who were formerly most generally elected by the people at the regular political elections, are still elected in twenty-nine states, but in an increasing number of states (thirteen) are appointed by the state boards of education; only in six states are they appointed by the Governor. The qualifications for such officials have risen since 1900 and most state-school officers hold graduate degrees. It is significant, however, that the qualifications required in those states where the positions are filled by appointment are normally higher than where popular election is the practice.

The chief state-school officer is the executive officer of the board and is tending to become a leader in the educational destinies of his state. He has general responsibility for advising his board on policy, for supervising the public schools to ensure the execution of legal requirements, for nominating the members of his staff, for preparing the budget, for approving plans for school buildings, for issuing teachers' certificates, for promoting or approving plans for creating larger administrative areas by consolidation, for preparing reports and other publications, and for distributing the state school funds with authority to withhold them from districts that do not comply with the legal requirements of the state.[11]

It is an accepted principle, however, that, while state departments of education should interest themselves in promoting higher standards and equalizing educational opportunities within their borders, the control should be limited to the requirement of minimum standards. In addition they should encourage local administrative units to go beyond the fundamental program and to adapt their work to local needs. The principle is a reaffirmation of the ideal of keeping educational concerns close to the people.

LOCAL CONTROL OF EDUCATION

On the principle discussed previously and because of long-established tradition, local areas (cities, towns, villages, rural districts, counties, and consolidated areas) have been entrusted by the constitutions or statutes of their states with the responsibility of administering their own systems of schools in accordance with the state laws and the regulations of the state education authorities. Hence, it is understood that the local areas carry out educational functions as a duty delegated to them by their respective states and under the control and supervision of those states so far as certain minimum standards are concerned. The people in each of the administrative areas have entrusted the administration of their educational affairs to school trustees or boards of education and their professional staffs. The members of the boards may be elected by popular vote or appointed by the mayors. In order to avoid the intrusion of partisan politics, the opinion of educators has come to favor elections separate from those held for other municipal affairs. In this way the hazards of frequent political changes and overturns can, it is expected, be avoided, and the educational issues — whether the election of board members or bond issues or buildings — be kept distinctly before the public. Further, in order to separate educational matters from other political issues and because the conduct of education is a state concern delegated to local authorities, the administration of education is considered not to be a municipal affair and the boards of education are regarded as agents of the states.

Controversies have arisen frequently on the question of the division of authority between education and city officials. Andrew S. Draper, Commissioner of Education of the State of New York, wrote in 1909: "The affairs of the school should be wholly separated from municipal business, and the school organization should have no connection whatever with municipal affairs. There is no ground for any connection between the two. The public-school system rests upon the taxing power of the state, and that is wholly within the control of the lawmaking power. The school system is a state system administered in the American fashion through representatives chosen by the people in their local surroundings or in any other way the state may direct. But these officers do not cease to be representatives of a state system, as was pointed out in the discussion of the legal basis of the schools, and there is every reason why their tenure and their powers should be wholly independent of municipal boards and officers." [12] That the principle stated by Commissioner Draper is still valid may be gathered from the following reference to the controversies on the subject. "These contentions have sometimes gone into the courts, and four or five hundred of such cases have been appealed to the highest legal tribunals. From the decisions of the courts in these cases there is available today an authoritative record which furnishes a pertinent and important illumination of the problems under consideration . . . The records show exceedingly few instances of municipal governments taking a position of leadership in promoting the welfare of education. It is not to be wondered at, therefore, that where litigation has arisen, the courts have most frequently held that education is a function of the state and that in the local administration of school the board of education representing the state is supreme." [13]

The same arguments have been put forward in favor of the fiscal independence of education authorities. It is asserted that the nature of the activities, the supplies, the records, and accounts involved in the conduct of education differ from the administration and conduct of other affairs of civil government. The necessity of coöperation with other divisions of government in preparing budgets and determining the amount to be raised by taxation has been recognized and approved, and tax limits within which the educational authorities can operate have been accepted. This point is made in a publication of the Educational Policies Commission in a discussion of fiscal independence of boards of education: "This does not mean that educational authorities are or should be indifferent to the demand that school budgets be made and school administration be conducted with reference to the total financial situation of the community or of the larger areas to which they may be related. In the best of jurisdictions school budgets are prepared with a view to the requirements of the other services and the financial resources available to all. In these jurisdictions school authorities are well informed respecting the state of general revenues and expenditures and do give to appropriate budget-making officers, as well as to the public, complete information to school receipts and outlays. They also seek information on the general situation from fiscal officers and invite from other specially qualified persons and the public a consideration of the tentative educational budget before reaching final determinations. This best practice should be more widely extended." [14]

The most important change in the character of the administrative authorities has been the reduction in the size of the education boards. At the beginning of the century, the boards in the larger administrative units represented geographical areas or wards and consisted of forty-five to fifty members. The prevailing practice at the end of the half century has come to favor a reduction in the size of boards to from five to nine members either elected at large by popular vote or appointed by the mayor. The members are elected for overlapping terms of four or five years and normally serve without pay. The advantages of the smaller board are that it can meet as a whole and need not break up into committees (except on special occasions), can more easily transact its business than a large body, and persons of higher caliber can be persuaded to serve, if elected or selected at large and not on local ward politics.

The board of education, representing the public, formulates the policies in coöperation with the state and is responsible for seeing that everything is done for the proper conduct of the school system and the provision of all the necessary services, such as suitable sites and buildings, equipment, school lunches, health of pupils, transportation if necessary, the preparation of the budget, and making appointments of the professional and lay staffs needed to operate the system. While the members may be expected to take an interest in the curricula and courses of study, their preparation has become a task that calls for more professional skill and competence than when their range and scope was clearly defined and limited. Perhaps the most important task of any board of education is to select and appoint a competent executive (superintendent or chief school officer), who is in turn responsible for recommending competent staff members and teachers for appointment by the boards. Ultimately, it is the responsibility of the executive officer and his staff to prepare policies and plans and to explain the needs of the school system to be considered and discussed by the board. But the public must also be heard both in the formulation of the policies and at the discussions of the board, whose meetings have tended to be open to the public.

There has been a notable change in the qualifications and duties of the school superintendent since 1900. At the beginning of the century, superintendents were chosen from the ranks of school principals or college professors or, at times, boards of education appointed one of their own members. There were no opportunities for special preparation for the job nor was there as yet available any serious literature on the problems of school administration other than annual reports of city and state boards of education, the character of which has already been mentioned, or a few books on school management. Facilities for the training of administrators began to be provided first at Teachers College, Columbia University, from about 1905. Mature students with experience in schools as teachers or principals began to open up the field with doctoral theses on various aspects of educational administration. The subject was rapidly expanded and became an important department in schools of education throughout the country. Opportunities for adding to the theoretical studies in the graduate courses were provided when professors of educational administration associated their students with themselves in the conduct of school surveys. The tendency was to require first a master's degree and later a doctorate for appointment to the position of superintendent;

in 1906 Wisconsin was the only state that required a special certificate for the position, a practice which had been adopted by thirty-three states in 1937.

A more recent development, following recommendations of the Association of Professors of School Administration, organized in 1947, has been an experiment in the recruiting, selection, and preparation of students for the field of educational administration. With a grant for five years from the W. K. Kellogg Foundation the experiment was started in 1950 at five centers serving their respective regions — Harvard University School of Education, Teachers College, Columbia University, University of Chicago, George Peabody College for Teachers, and the University of Texas School of Education. The essential aspect of the scheme is coöperation with the school systems of each region, theoretical study in the professional institutions, and a period of internship in an administrative office.

For a time there was a tendency to separate the educational functions from the business functions of administration. This separation did not work satisfactorily and, early in the century, the principle was adopted of consolidating all the functions in the hands of the administrator responsible for the supervision of all activities pertaining to education, with specialists in such matters as business and accounting, public relations, buildings, records and research, school supervision, tests and measurements, personnel, and curriculum, and special subjects under and responsible to him.

There has thus been a considerable expansion in the duties of the superintendent's office since the beginning of the century. Not only has there been an expansion of duties, but there has also developed a call for men with broader vision and competence, which cannot, however, be developed by training. While there has been a shift from the bureaucratic methods, common earlier in the century before the supply of better trained and better educated teachers increased, there is a tendency to develop routine methods and paper work. The disappearance of bureaucratic methods is by no means complete, but more opportunities have been provided for the participation of teachers in discussing policies and in making contributions in the fields of their competence. Nevertheless, it would not be incorrect to say that there has been a general leveling in education. The days seem to have gone when certain systems could be looked to as examples to be studied for quality of standards or for innovations worthy of notice. The reputation of individual superintendents made the reputation of a school system. At the same time, the career of a superintendent has become less hazardous than it was in the first quarter of the century, even though his appointment continues to be for a term of years and without that security of tenure which teachers have achieved in most parts of the country.

The position of the superintendent of schools bears a closer resemblance to that of the executive of a business corporation than to that of a profession. The pattern of educational administration has, in fact, been likened to that of a business career: the board of education is the board of directors, the superintendent is the executive officer, with a staff of lesser executives under him to define and supervise the activities of the employes or the teachers, and the public is the body of stockholders who hold the board and the superintendent accountable.

EXPANDING THE UNITS OF ADMINISTRATION

Although a considerable number of administrative units remain which can only afford to provide an elementary school with one teacher in charge (nearly 59,700 in 1949–50), there has been a definite trend in the direction of developing larger administrative units with enough taxable wealth to maintain not only graded primary but also high schools, to secure better qualified and better paid teachers, to provide a wider range of equipment, books, and amenities, including playgrounds and school lunches, and to provide for the transportation of pupils living within a range of as much as twenty miles distance from the school. The development of larger administrative units has been made possible by the provision of better roads and improved means of transportation of children to and from school. But in the last analysis it has been found that the amalgamation or consolidation of school districts can only become effective if supported by public opinion as expressed by the votes of the public, which tends to be somewhat stubborn in surrendering its right to maintain its own school, however modest it may be. Consolidation cannot be brought about, as history has shown, by state fiat.

The administration of the single elementary school with one or two teachers is simple and is generally conducted by the elected school trustees. At one time, before the number of school districts began to be reduced in the second quarter of the century, there were more school trustees in some states than there were teachers in their schools. The advantage of the larger units lies not merely in the improvement of the teaching personnel and of instruction, but in the employment of qualified administrators as superintendents or as supervising principals and the election of school board members over a larger area. Something may be lost in the disappearance of "the little red schoolhouse," it is charged, and in removing the control of education from the taxpayers of a local district, but the interests of the children, who benefit from a better education, are paramount. Time must be allowed for the transfer of public understanding and coöperation from the old one-teacher school to the larger consolidated school.

From the national point of view the improvement of rural education assumed particular significance in a period of social and economic transition that occurred after World War I. Changes have taken place in the nation's economy and in the distribution of the population. To the increase of the urban population the migration from the rural areas has contributed and continues to contribute its share. The fear has frequently been expressed that the standards of citizenship in urban communities in general may decline as a consequence of the influx of people from the rural areas who have not had the advantage of a good education. The Advisory Committee on Education, appointed in 1936 by President F. D. Roosevelt, included the following statement in one of its reports: "If, for a long period, each succeeding generation is drawn in large numbers from those areas in which economic conditions are poorest, if the population of the Nation continues to be recruited largely from economically underprivileged groups, and if the inability of the depressed economic areas and groups to provide proper education for their children is not corrected by aid from areas and groups more prosperous, the effect on American civilization and on representative political institutions may be disastrous." [15] While not specifically mentioned here, the effect of rural migration on urban standards is often referred to by sociologists.[16]

THE ORDEAL OF WARS AND DEPRESSION

The issue is only part of a larger national movement which is concerned with the degree to which equality of educational opportunity, the corollary of the traditional American faith in education, is actually being provided. The issue only began to be recognized during World War I, when the inadequate standards of education of the draftees were discovered, and after the war when as a result of the economic conditions and the increasing enrollments in the high schools it began to be realized that education was still the nation's unfinished business. The increased enrollments in the high schools was inspired by the success of high school and college graduates in the armed forces and the publication by the U. S. Bureau of

Education of a bulletin on *The Money Value of Education* (1917).

The era of uncertainty about the American educational system and the realization of the ideal of equality of educational opportunity came in the 'thirties. The period of the depression followed by the years of World War II was a time of stocktaking, a period in which the educational needs met and unmet were surveyed nationally and by states. Plans for meeting the needs as yet unmet had hardly been drawn up when new problems arose consequent to the unanticipated rise in the birth rate during and after World War II. The shortage of school buildings and classrooms and of teachers created a serious situation which is yet to be solved.

The depression years of the 'thirties were years of a downward trend in education. For the first time in the century there was a decline in expenditures. In many parts of the country, schools were not opened for lack of funds or were operated for short terms. Capital outlays were reduced to a minimum, and the building and repair of schools were held up until federal grants were made available under the Federal Emergency Administration of Public Works (P.W.A.) and the Works Progress Administration (W.P.A.). There was a drop in the per capita costs per pupil, and salaries were reduced or in some cases not paid at all. Many teachers and prospective teachers joined the ranks of the unemployed. Paradoxically, there was a phenomenal increase in the number of students in high schools from 3,787,466 in 1926 to 8,719,000 in 1932 — driven to enter school because of lack of employment opportunities and assisted by grants under the National Youth Administration (N.Y.A.) scheme.

Financial assistance to the states and local administrative authorities was provided under emergency regulations distributed by various administrative agencies in the federal government, some new, others already in existence. The federal Emergency Relief Administration (F.E.R.A.) provided funds for the employment of teachers, the organization of adult education courses and literacy classes, the provision of vocational education for unemployed adults, and the establishment of nursery schools for the care of the health, nutrition, play, social life, and mental and physical hygiene of young children.

In 1934, to enable young persons between sixteen and twenty-four to continue their education in high schools, colleges, and graduate schools the F.E.R.A. provided grants. In the following year, the National Youth Administration was established as an autonomous agency under the Works Progress Administration (W.P.A.) to administer such grants for the employment of youth to enable them to pursue their regular studies in high schools, colleges, and graduate schools. The amount of the grants was at first $6 a month for students in high schools, $15 in colleges, and $25 in graduate schools, in return for work which was of value to the institutions or the communities where they were located and which would otherwise not be done. In 1939 the N.Y.A. was transferred to the Federal Security Agency (F.S.A.) with an enlarged program "to extend the educational opportunities of the youth of the country and to bring them through the processes of training into the possession of skills which enable them to find employment." New centers were established in which students divided their time equally between production and service projects and attendance at classes. The schools were federally administered and controlled.

One year before the N.Y.A. went into operation, the Civilian Conservation Corps (C.C.C.) was established for youths between seventeen and twenty-one, "for the relief of unemployment and for the performance of useful work and other purposes." The youth enrolled were sent to camps in groups of two-hundred and were engaged mainly in conservation projects under the direction of the War Department. The education which was intended to be part of the scheme was inadequate until the C.C.C., like the N.Y.A. was transferred in 1939 to the F.S.A. The experiment of the C.C.C. was considered to be useful and in some quarters it was thought that it could be developed as a type of secondary education for students who could not adjust themselves to the current programs of study.

Although they were regarded as important measures for relief of youth in an emergency crisis, criticisms of both the C.C.C. and N.Y.A. mounted. They centered mainly on the fact that both schemes were administered directly by agencies of the federal government and encroached on the rights of the States in the field of education. Many of the leading colleges and universities refused to accept the benefits of N.Y.A. because control and regulations were entirely in the federal agency administering the scheme. By those concerned with the administration of public-school education the criticisms were prompted by the fear that the encroachment on the states' rights, even in an emergency, might threaten the established principles of federal-state relations in education.[17]

The mistake of the depression period was not repeated. When the more serious emergency of World War II engulfed the country and the activities of the U. S. Office of Education were extended in all directions needed for training civilian war workers and for maintaining national morale, the Office worked in close coöperation with the state and local authorities except in a few areas where vocational training courses had to be established *ad hoc*. Insofar as the elementary and secondary schools are concerned, under the leadership of the U. S. Office of Education, the National Education Association and its many affiliates, especially the Educational Policies Commission, and the state and local administrative agencies, they were dedicated before Pearl Harbor to programs of Education for National Defense and after Pearl Harbor to Education for Victory. The chief problem was to stem the exodus from the high schools of pupils who were attracted by the opportunities for remunerative work to meet the manpower shortage. At the same time a serious situation was created by a shortage of teachers who entered the armed services or else took advantage of the many better paid jobs that were readily available. Of the two immediate effects of the war the more serious and more lasting one was the shortage of teachers and the reduction in the number of prospective teachers, a phenomenon that was to endure for years after the war and to become increasingly acute as the enrollments in the elementary and later in the high schools increased at a rate that was not at first anticipated.

The effects of the war and postwar years on capital expenditures for buildings and repairs were not fully felt until some ten years after the end of the war. School buildings fell into disrepair; new buildings could not be erected because of the shortage of necessary materials and manpower. There was no moratorium in the rapid increase in the number of children to be educated, however, and the shortage of buildings and teachers were legacies of World War II that constituted a major problem to be solved in the second half of the century. The other problem arose from the competition between the federal, state, and local governments for their share in the taxes, with the advantage resting on the side of the federal government.

INEQUALITIES IN EDUCATIONAL OPPORTUNITIES

These problems, however, were not inherently new. They had become more serious because there was a widespread realization that the schools alone could provide the best preparation for future citizens of the nation to meet the challenges of the times in a continuous war of ideas. It was also realized that a major principle of democracy is to recognize the worth and dignity of every individual and that this recognition should be implemented by providing equality of educational opportunity for every boy and girl regardless of the economic circumstances of their parents and their places of residence.

The war years provided an even better opportunity than the depression period for taking stock of the situation and planning for the future. The studies that were undertaken were, in fact, a continuation of those begun before the war. In a report on *Equal Opportunity for Youth: a National Responsibility*, prepared for the American Youth Commission of the American Council on Education and published in 1938, Dr. Newton Edwards wrote that fifteen states provided an education that cost less than was necessary for a minimum defensible program of instruction, estimated at that time to be $60 per pupil. The range was from $24 per pupil in Arkansas to $124 in New York. The reason for the disparity lay in the difference in the distribution of the taxable wealth and the number of children to be educated. It was pointed out that the problem was national in scope because of the internal migration and mobility of the people, increased by the movement of industry, and the dependence of urban industrial areas upon the rural areas for population growth.

The failure of boys and girls to take advantage of opportunities for secondary education for economic reasons has been emphasized for many years. In 1922 Dr. George S. Counts had already discussed in *The Selective Character of Secondary Education*, findings which were confirmed and amplified in the report of the National Survey of Secondary Education conducted under the U. S. Office of Education (1932), in Howard M. Bell's *Youth Tell Their Story* (1938), in the report of the New York State Regents' Inquiry (1939) and in *Who Shall be Educated: the Challenge of Unequal Opportunities* (1944) by W. Lloyd Warner, Robert Havighurst, and M. B. Loeb.

In 1945 two important studies were published, one showing the widespread existence of inequalities in education and the other indicating the effect of these inequalities on the nation's economic and social problems. The first of these studies, *Unfinished Business: An Inventory of Public School Expenditures in the United States* was prepared by Dr. John K. Norton and Dr. Eugene S. Lawlor for the U. S. Office of Education, the American Council on Education, and the National Education Association. Data were quoted showing that 3,000,000 adults had never attended school, that 10,000,-000 were virtually illiterate, and that 2,000,000 children of school age were not attending school. Selective Service figures showed that nearly 5,000,000 men had to be rejected for educational, physical, and mental deficiencies. Children were taught in school buildings ranging from one-room shacks with relatively unprepared teachers and inadequate equipment to palatial buildings with up-to-date equipment and instructional materials and taught by competent teachers. The cost per classroom unit, including teachers' salaries, books, equipment and maintenance in 1939 ranged from $6,000 to less than $100. For the country as a whole the median cost per classroom unit per year was $1,600. The lowest expenditures were found in those areas which had the largest number of children to educate. The poorer states made the greater efforts to raise funds for the support of schools and devoted a larger percentage of their income to education than did the wealthy states. Thus, Mississippi devoted 3.4 per cent of the state's income to education, but the expenditure per classroom unit was only $400 per year as contrasted with an expenditure of $4,100 per classroom unit in New York at a cost of 3.61 per cent of her income devoted to education.

The second report, prepared by the Committee on Education of the United States Chamber of Commerce, was entitled *Education: An Investment in People*. The report showed that 80 per cent of those who went to college and beyond, 39 per cent of those who had attended high school or graduated, and 11 per cent of those who had only com-

pleted eight grades reached the $5,000 a year income bracket.
Similar data were presented on the relation of the level of
educational expenditure in a state and the amount of education completed by its citizens and (1) rent paid, (2) the
volume of economic activity, (3) per capita retail sales, (4)
the number of telephones per 1,000 of the population, and
(5) the circulation of national magazines. The committee
concluded that "business must recognize the value of an expanded education for economic improvement" and to meet
the popular demand for "a fuller participation in the larger
life."

FEDERAL GOVERNMENT AND EDUCATION

All the studies pointed to the pooling of the resources of
the nation — federal, state, and local — to be used for the
removal of inequalities in education. This need had already
been emphasized in 1938 in the report of President Roosevelt's Advisory Committee. Appointed in 1936 to make a
study of the experience under the existing program of federal
aid for vocational education which had been provided under
the Smith-Hughes Act of 1917, the committee was requested
in 1937 to extend its inquiry into the whole subject of federal
relations to state and local education. It wrote in its report:

The inequalities of educational opportunity that characterize
the educational system today constitute a challenge to American
statesmanship. For millions of children the opportunity for anything more than the smallest amount of meager and formal public
education is largely determined by place of birth. In communities
where there are the fewest children and the most wealth, education is supported liberally. In communities where there are the
most children and the least wealth, necessarily the local support
of education is far below an adequate level. . .
    The people of America are our most important resource. What-
ever may happen to the conservation or the destruction of our
material resources, nothing completely disastrous is likely to happen to a healthy and intelligent people, and nothing but disaster

can happen if we are unable to meet successfully the strains and problems of our world.

The Nation's future depends on the quality of the American people. Within the limits of practical action and available resources, the Nation should see to it that the next step be taken to give all the people opportunity to develop their capacities to the full, for their own benefit individually and for the best interests of the country as a whole.[18]

On the basis of experience of federal activities in education during World War II, which were viewed with alarm as a drift to centralization, the Problems and Policies Committee of the American Council on Education and the Educational Policies Commission of the National Education Association made the following statement of principles:

Adequate organization for the provision of fair educational opportunity for all children and youth will require some participation of the federal government in education. The experience of a hundred and fifty years of national life, the compulsion of modern social demands, and the probable character of the period which lies ahead, all testify that federal participation in education in the United States is a permanent phenomenon. Federal participation in education is no longer a debate. It has become a fact.

The issue which still has to be settled is: Can federal participation in education be kept within proper bounds and limits, or will it eventually swallow up all education in a system of centralized control and administration?

The basic control of education can be kept in the states and localities with the federal government assisting in the development of this service but refraining from dominating it, providing the issue involved in federal-state relations in education are clearly understood and providing sound principles are formulated and observed in guiding the evolution of this important relationship.[19]

Although the federal government began to provide aid for education soon after the establishment of the Republic, the early grants of land under the Ordinances of 1785 and 1787 were given outright to the states for the use of public schools.

Subsequent legislation was in the form of grants for colleges of agricultural and mechanical arts and later for agricultural experiment stations. Federal aid for public school education is not mentioned by Cubberley in his *Public Education in the United States*, published in 1919, until he refers to the unsuccessful Davis bill (1907) and the Page bill (1912) which preceded the enactment of the Smith-Hughes Act (1917) to provide federal funds to the states for vocational education. The Smith-Hughes Act itself was the culmination of a report of the President's Commission appointed in 1913 to inquire into vocational education. In 1914 the Smith-Lever Act aided public education through grants which have been administered by the Department of Agriculture to provide extension classes for adults for the improvement of agriculture and rural farm life. The grants under both acts have been increased by amending acts. It was believed, however, that such grants were for specific purposes and that what was needed was the coöperation of Federal Government to assist in the removal of inequalities in education generally.

Federal funds, as already mentioned, were made available for education during the depression and war years. They were granted piecemeal without any discernible policy behind them. They did not contribute to the general advantage of the public-school systems. Nor was there any uniform plan of administration or of distributing grants; almost every agency in the federal government was engaged in some educational activity. To develop a policy and to secure unification in administration the Educational Policies Commission in 1945 recommended an effective Office of Education to exercise leadership in education, to deal with the states in federal-state relationships, to conduct investigations and research, to convene conferences of lay and professional leaders in education as well as to continue to collect and publish statistical and other information on education throughout the country. A year earlier, at a meeting of the National Education Association, it was recommended that there should be created a federal department of Health, Education, and Welfare under a secretary with a seat in the Cabinet. The recommendation was not put into effect until 1952.

Since World War I, bills have been presented in nearly every session of Congress proposing the provision of federal funds for education but they have always been defeated. The chief opposition has come from those who feared centralization and the encroachment of the federal government on states' rights by the exercise of control and dictation in educational affairs. The fear was not without cause, for some years elapsed before a tendency in that direction, manifested by the Federal Board for Vocational Education to control the character of vocational education, was checked. Nor was the experience under the emergency measures adopted in the periods of the depression and World War II reassuring. The issue of states' rights and fear of centralized control were probably factors that were more influential in the rejection of proposals to enact federal aid laws than the second source of opposition. The private and parochial schools which were always excluded from the benefits of such proposals resisted the measures. To some extent another group that stood in opposition to federal aid to the states objected on the ground that the measures provided for the equal treatment of white and colored children in the distribution of funds granted to the states.

It was not until 1945 that the chances of the successful enactment of a federal-aid law seemed to be brighter. In August of that year, Senator Robert A. Taft proposed that a bill should be included in the program for the next session of Congress to provide federal aid "to enable the poorer states to provide a minimum of education for every child." In November, Senator Robert Ramspeck of Georgia invited a bipartisan group to meet in Washington to sponsor a bill for federal aid. Following the meeting a Committee for the

Support of Federal Aid for Public Schools was formed. The conditions seemed to be favorable and it was expected that a federal-aid bill would at last be enacted. In his Annual Message to Congress on January 21, 1946, President Truman reiterated an earlier proposal which he had made that federal aid should be provided to the states to assure "more nearly equal opportunities for a good education." He ended his message with the following statement: "The Federal Government has not sought and will not seek to dominate education in the states. It should continue its historic role of leadership and advice and, for the purposes of equalizing educational opportunities, it should extend further financial support to the cause of education in areas where this is desirable."

This principle has been embodied in more recent bills to provide federal aid for education, and the exercise of any direction, supervision, or control over or prescription with respect to any agency in receipt of funds has been specifically prohibited. The bill which had the support of the bipartisan committee was not passed.

The fact that federal aid must some time be provided for education if the ideal of equality of opportunity is ever to be realized has been established beyond contradiction. There is no doubt, however, that any measure that can in any way be interpreted as a tendency to control and direct the purposes and content of education would meet with considerable opposition as contrary to the American tradition that education is the concern of the people and must be administered by states and localities. Further, remote determination of what shall be done in a school or school system is contrary to the pedagogical principle that instruction must be adapted to the environment with which pupils are familiar and be expanded therefrom. The fact is that a consistent policy for federal aid has not been developed either on supervising the administration of the funds to be appropriated to the states or on the methods to be employed in the distribution of funds —

whether on the basis of population or of children of school age or of the needs of the several states. At the end of the first half of the century nothing was clearer than the fact that not even the wealthiest states could meet the increasing cost of education except by coöperation on a national front but without the sacrifice of traditional principles of administration.

OUTLOOK FOR THE POSTWAR YEARS AND NATIONAL LEADERSHIP

The postwar financial needs to provide education in the country were estimated in 1943 when the National Resources Board drafted its proposals for a postwar program for education. The program was to include education for health and safety, vocational training, education for leisure, home and family living, national security and citizenship, and social and economic education. The program was also to provide opportunities for those whose education had been interrupted by the war and the retraining of men and women demobilized from the armed forces and defense industries. The total cost of the proposed program was estimated to be $6,100,000,000, or slightly more than twice the total expenditure for education by all public agencies in 1940 which amounted to $2,817,000,000.

The outstanding needs of American education that were considered urgent at the close of the war were presented in the following summary in *Proposals for Public Education in Postwar America*, issued by the National Education Association in 1944: (1) wider application of the principle that an acceptable minimum of educational opportunity should be available to every individual regardless of his status; (2) general improvement of programs to develop physical and mental health; (3) greater emphasis upon intelligent self-direction in study and learning; (4) increased opportunity for learning how to do, particularly through work experience in vocational programs; (5) increased opportunity for learning and practicing the ways of democratic group living; (6) more systematic adaption of teaching methods, content, and length of schooling to individual and social needs; (7) broader cultural background and greater technical knowledge and skill on the part of all professional staff members; (8) reorganization and enlargement of local school districts and the integration of state educational facilities in the interest of efficient and economical school programs; (9) general acceptance of the principle that public education should receive its financial support from all levels of government, state, and national.

There does not exist in the United States a central governmental agency that can control or even define the scope and purposes of education. Nevertheless, in addition to the numerous organizations that give expression to public and professional opinion, a medium has been created for the general discussion, from a national point of view, of problems affecting the welfare of children. This has been done at intervals of about ten years by White House Conferences. The Conference held in 1909 was devoted to a consideration of The Care of Dependent Children and led through its recommendations to the creation in 1912 of the Children's Bureau in the Department of Labor, later transferred to the Federal Security Agency, and more recently to the Department of Health, Education, and Welfare. In 1919 a Conference was held on Child Welfare. In 1930 the Conference dealt with Child Health and Protection, and in The Children's Charter which was then drawn up there were emphasized the importance of prenatal and postnatal care of mothers, protection of child health from birth through adolescence, health instruction, measures for the protection and care of physically and mentally handicapped children, the care of delinquent children, protection of every child against labor conditions detrimental to health and welfare, and an education adapted to a child's abilities and given a preparation for life and "for a living which will yield him the maximum of satisfaction." Children in a democracy was the theme of the Conference held in 1940, which, among other things, recommended the creation of larger units of attendance and administration in order "to broaden the base of financial support and to make possible a modern well-equipped school for any child at a reasonable per capita cost"; to reduce inequalities of opportunity in education it was recommended that the tax burdens be equalized by state grants to local authorities and by federal aid to the states. The Conference on Rural Education in 1944 produced The Charter of Education for Rural Children which recommended that local areas of administration should be large enough to provide all the services of modern educational systems and to guarantee an American standard of educational opportunity through the coöperation of the community, the state, and the nation in providing the financial basis. According to the charter, educational opportunities include access to education in modern school buildings for nine months a year as the right of every child, health services, vocational guidance, library facilities, recreational activities, and transportation, and school lunches where necessary.

The issues continued to multiply for reasons mentioned earlier — the unprecedented birth rate during and after World War II. This had produced a large number of problems not previously anticipated in plans for postware education — the shortage of teachers and buildings, oversize classes and double sessions, the complex problems of secondary education, the employment of substandard teachers, and the failure of teachers' salaries to keep up with the rising cost of living. The White House Conference convened by President Eisenhower to meet in November 1955, was a conference on education rather than a conference on some specific aspect of education, as had been those held previously. The issues discussed were the following: (1) What should our schools accomplish? (2) In what way can we organize our schools more efficiently and economically? (3) What are our school building needs? (4) How can we get enough good teachers — and keep them? (5) How can we finance our schools — build and operate them? (6) How can we obtain a continuing public interest in education? It will be noted that the last question justifies the title and emphasis of this Chapter: that the American principle is that education is primarily a concern of the public and that it is dependent upon the understanding and confidence of the public.

CHARACTERISTICS OF THE AMERICAN EDUCATIONAL SYSTEM

By the middle of the twentieth century the outstanding characteristics of the American educational system had been clearly established. The system is based on the principles that it must be classless, coeducational, nonpartisan in politics, and secular. The organizational pattern was clear and definite. The nursery school was slowly beginning to be recognized as an important and valuable social and educational institution to be added to the public-school system. The kindergarten had already spread and had won an established place for itself in the larger school systems. The articulation between the preschool and the early grades of the primary school and between the elementary grades and the high school had been considerably improved, whether the systems consisted of the preschool-8-4 plan or the preschool-6-3-3 plan, and no longer constituted a problem as it did in the early years of the century. Another reorganization on the lines of a 6-4-4 plan, adding two years of junior college on to the high-school years, has been proposed and tried but is not likely to be adopted for many years, although the number of junior colleges will probably increase as independent institutions within the public school systems.

There was more clarity in the middle of the century about the organization of the school systems than there seemed to be assurance about the aims and purposes for which they were created, that is, about the educational objectives. The first issue discussed at the White House Conference on Education, held in November 1955, as already mentioned was "What should our schools accomplish? " The question appeared to indicate that, after nearly fifty years of extensive discussion and the growth of a vast educational literature, the issue still remained unsettled. The guess may be hazarded that the issue had not arisen anew because of the cultural changes that had taken place and continued to take place, or because of the political situation and the challenge to democracy, or because of the international position in which the nation finds itself.

The first principle of the American school system is that it must be classless, a principle which involves a consideration first, of the existence of dual systems in the Southern states, and, second, of the increase in the number of private or non-public schools. Under the dual system, separate schools have been maintained in seventeen states and the District of Columbia for white and Negro children. In 1899–1900 the number of Negro children of school age in those states was 2,991,100 and of these 1,539,507 or 51.46 per cent were enrolled in schools for colored children as compared with 68.28 per cent enrolled in schools for white children. The enrollments in the schools for Negro pupils began to rise rapidly in 1949–50 as did those for white pupils both in elementary and high schools. The average daily attendance of the pupils enrolled rose from 81.1 per cent in 1945–46 to 85.3 per cent in 1949–50. The average length of school terms in 1949–50 was 173 days, while the average number of days attended by each pupil enrolled advanced from 97 days in 1929–30 to 147.9 days in 1949–50. In the ten Southern states and the District of Columbia reporting on the subject, the salaries of Negro teachers was lower and in some cases considerably lower than for white teachers, but in four instances they compared quite favorably. A new era was ushered in when the United States

Supreme Court on May 17, 1954, declared that the segregation of white and Negro pupils in separate schools was unconstitutional.[20]

The second issue concerns the place of private or nonpublic schools, both elementary and secondary and became particularly serious in the last decade of the half century because of the increase in their numbers and enrollments. The latter increased from 2,723,666 (2,232,251 elementary and 403,415 secondary) in 1931–32 to 3,288,426 (2,662,920 elementary and 625,506 secondary) in 1949–50. The percentage of pupils in private schools rose from 8.10 per cent in 1899–1900 to about 10 per cent in 1950.

The average American, when he thinks of education below the college level, always thinks of it in terms of the public school, and for that reason the increase in the number of private schools came as a surprise. The term nonpublic school covers a variety of types of private schools. It includes: (1) experimental schools, sometimes incorporated and under the control of a board of trustees and sometimes proprietary; (2) boarding schools; (3) "finishing" schools for girls; and (4) preparatory schools; and (5) denominational or parochial schools. Many institutions in the first four groups are members of the National Council of Independent Schools and prefer to be known as "independent" rather than as "private" schools.

The reasons for the establishment of nonpublic schools vary; some owe their existence to parents' dissatisfaction with the work of the public schools, and the large classes that have developed, and to the fact that pupils are drawn from many cultural and economic backgrounds to the possible detriment of their children's language and manners; other schools have been patronized because it was thought that their discipline was better than it has become in the public schools and that their programs were more definitely directed to preparing pupils for entrance to college. The large majority of nonpublic schools are denominational or parochial, and of these most are Roman Catholic; the number of Protestant parochial schools is about one-third the number of the Roman Catholic schools and the majority are maintained by Seventh Day Adventists and Lutherans; the number of Jewish parochial schools is considerably smaller than the number of the others but has grown in the past twenty years.

The Roman Catholic parochial schools have been established in the conviction that education cannot be of any value unless it is permeated in all aspects by religious values, and those the values of the Church. For this reason the Church is opposed to public schools, which over a century ago began to be nonsectarian and secular and which are regarded by their critics at best as neutral and at worst as godless or atheistic. The number of Roman Catholic parochial schools in 1949–50 was 10,778 (8,589 elementary and 2,189 secondary) with a total enrollment of 3,086,387 pupils (2,560,-815 in elementary and 505,572 in secondary schools), constituting 93 per cent of the total number enrolled in nonpublic (private and parochial) schools in the country.

It is a recognized principle in the United States that parents have the right to choose the school to which they wish to send their children provided they are willing to pay the necessary fees. The state is not entitled to exercise a monopoly in education. It may under its compulsory laws and regulations require children to be educated, but it cannot compel them to attend a public school. This was an established principle in law when it was challenged in the years following World War I. In Michigan it was proposed in 1920 and 1924 to amend the state constitution so as to abolish all private schools; the move was defeated on both occasions by a referendum vote of about two to one. But in Oregon a compulsory education law was enacted compelling parents to send their children between the ages of eight and sixteen to public schools. This would have meant the closing of all nonpublic schools including parochial schools. Action was brought against the state by a private military school and by a Roman Catholic teaching order and was carried to the United States Supreme Court. In 1925 the Court, in the case of *Pierce v. Society of the Sisters of Jesus and Mary* (268 U.S. 510,1925), declared the law to be unconstitutional, and among other points in the decision laid down the following principle: "The fundamental theory of liberty under which the governments in this Union reposes excludes any general power of the state to standardize its children by forcing them to accept instruction from public teachers only. The child is not the mere creature of the state; those who nurture him and direct his destiny have the right, coupled with the duty, to recognize and prepare him for additional obligations." At the same time the Court confirmed the right of the state to supervise and inspect nonpublic schools particularly in matters of compulsory attendance, competence of teachers, who should be "of good moral character and patriotic disposition," and to insist upon the inclusion of "certain studies plainly essential to good citizenship," and the absence of instruction "which is manifestly inimical to the public welfare." The Court thus confirmed the practice of most states in relation to nonpublic education.

The nonpublic schools became an issue because it was felt that such schools are divisive and that the development of national unity requires that all children of all classes and creeds should be educated together for some years in the same schools. No evidence was adduced that nonpublic schools had in fact been divisive, except for a few adult education centers which were found to be politically oriented in a left-wing direction. Undoubtedly the common public school did prove to be an effective institution for the Americanization of the heterogeneous masses that make up the population of the country. Nevertheless, the problem of inculcating mutual respect and understanding between children and adults of groups that differ on account of social, economic, racial, and religious reasons, and differ as between native-born and foreign-born continued to be serious. It was the recognition of the seriousness of this problem that stimulated the development of programs of intergroup and intercultural education and education for better human relations. It was realized that tensions caused by interracial and interreligious conflicts in the years of the depression and of World War II were inimical to the successful achievement of the democratic ideal. A movement was launched in Springfield, Mass., in the 'forties to promote intercultural education in the schools. The movement spread to other school systems and was sponsored by several national organizations.[21]

The Roman Catholic hierarchy, however, felt that the existence of parochial schools was challenged because there had been an increase in their number and enrollments. To some extent this increase is resented because it is felt that the Roman Catholics have been among the chief opponents of federal aid for education which in all bills proposed has always been restricted to public schools. On the other hand, it is argued that the constitutional provision on the separation of Church and State has been violated because parochial and other nonpublic schools not run for profit are tax-exempt. The same issue came up in the matter of textbooks and transportation for parochial school pupils at public expense. In the case of *Cochran v. Board of Education of Louisiana* the United States Supreme Court decided that the provision of textbooks to parochial school pupils at public expense was legal (281 U.S. 370, 1930), and in *Everson v. Board of Education of the Township of Ewing, N.J., et al.*, that free transportation of such children was not unconstitutional (320 U.S. 1, 1947). The grounds for those decisions were that such provisions were for the children's benefit and that the grants were not made to the school that they attended. During World War II grants were made under some of the emergency measures, as indicated earlier, to nonpublic schools and created a great deal of concern as possibly establishing a precedent for the future in the matter of federal aid for education.

The position of American educators on nonpublic schools was stated by the Educational Policies Commission in the following passage: "No one would deny to the parents the acceptance of their obligation to provide religious education for their children. Most of our citizens would urge that this education be provided by the home and by the church while leaving to the public school system the provision of secular education. If we acknowledge that education is a function of the state then we should seek to develop a school system good enough for all and adequate to meet the needs of all our citizens." [21] The fear was expressed that the establishment of nonpublic schools would divert the interest of citizens from the public schools. The fear that "the greater the proportion of our youth who fail to attend our public schools, the greater the threat to our democratic unity" [22] was also expressed by Dr. James Bryant Conant, then President of Harvard University, in an address to the American Association of School Administrators at its meeting in Boston in 1952. His comment aroused considerable opposition from Roman Catholic leaders.

The argument for parochial schools — and in this the Roman Catholics are joined by other denominations, Protestant and Jewish, although the number of non-Catholic parochial schools is relatively small — rests on the fact that the public schools are secular. The reasons why the American school system began to become secular over a century ago seem to have been forgotten by those who are inclined to call these schools godless or atheistic, or at best neutral, a charge which Commissioner Draper felt called upon to refute when he wrote his book on *American Education* in 1909. The movement to supplement the work of the public schools by the

provision and improvement of religious education outside the
schools began in 1903 when the Religious Education Association was formed "to keep before the public the ideal of religious education and the sense of its need and value." The
Association devoted its efforts to the improvement of instruction in Sunday schools and to the promotion of released time
for religious education. The practice of releasing pupils from
their public schools for one period a week to attend religious
instruction classes organized in their respective churches was
first introduced in Gary, Ind., in 1913. The movement developed slowly, but the agitation for religious education became stronger after World War I in the face of what was
regarded as a general decline of faith, of growing materialism
in education as in life, of increasing juvenile delinquency, and
of relaxation of discipline in the home and in the school, for
which the pragmatic philosophy of education was blamed.
In 1946 released time was permitted in 2200 communities
under legal sanctions in twenty-four states. The constitution-
ality of released time was challenged in the courts. In the
case of *Vashti McCollum v. Board of Education of School
District 71, Champaign, Ill.*, the United States Supreme Court,
by a decision of eight to one, declared it to be unconstitutional to give released time religious instruction on public
school premises (333 U.S. 203, 1948). In *Zorach v. Board of
Education of New York City*, the United States Supreme
Court, by a decision of six to three, declared that released
time was not unconstitutional if given on premises outside
the public schools (343 U.S. 306, 1948).

Released time, however, is considered to be an unsatisfactory method of meeting the issue of religious education.
In 1944 the American Council on Education called a conference on Religion and Public Education at Princeton, N.J.:
"in order to clarify the issues raised in recent discussions of
this subject in educational circles, in the press, and in various
public and private groups." In 1947 the Council published a

report of the committee on *The Relation of Religion to Public Education: Basic Principles*. The committee declared that it was the responsibility of the public schools "to give the young an understanding of the culture and an appreciation of the ideals, values, and institutions which the culture cherishes," and to acquaint them with the role of religion in the culture. The committee insisted, however, that "public education may not propagate religious dogmas or arbitrate religious differences"; its function is rather to "create a sensitive awareness of the religious resources upon which men have learned to rely." To this end school curricula might include instruction in the religions of the world and in that way not only carry out the aims of the committee but also develop mutual respect between members of different religions and different cultures.

The leaders in public school education met the challenge of godlessness by affirmations that the place of religion in American democracy was recognized in the public schools and that nothing was done to undermine the faith of the pupils. They rejected the notion that a common core of religion, acceptable to the members of all creeds, could be found and they also rejected the introduction of sectarianism into the public schools. They might have mentioned that the reading of the Bible was required in fifteen states and permitted in twenty-five states and that high-school students could receive credit for Bible study. Emphasis was placed by the spokesmen for public education on the fact that the moral and spiritual education of pupils had always been one of the purposes of education.

In a report on the subject issued by the Educational Policies Commission in 1951, *Moral and Spiritual Values in Public Schools*, the general principle was stated as follows: "The teaching of moral and spiritual values in the public schools of the United States must be done without endangering religious freedom and without circumventing the policy of church and state. Our society leaves to the home and the church the responsibility for instruction designed to secure the acceptance of religious faith. Thus the home, the church, and the school each share in moral and spiritual development, while each may make the contribution to that development for which it is peculiarly fitted.

"The development of moral and spiritual values is basic to all other educational objectives. Education uninspired by moral and spiritual values is directionless." [24] To this end the commission recommended that moral and spiritual values should permeate every aspect of the school curriculum and be woven into the entire life of the school as a vital part of all subjects of instruction in the school program.

It seems unlikely that any proposal for denominational education in public schools is likely to meet with success since there is a tradition of over a century that the schools shall be common to all the children of all the people. Nor would it be possible to accommodate the demands for their particular sectarian beliefs that might be put forward by the more than two hundred and fifty denominations of the country.

The final characteristic of the American schools is that they should be nonpartisan is strictly maintained in the sense that they are not used for propaganda in favor of one or other of the major political parties. But the term nonpartisan has been very broadly interpreted. As a result efforts, particularly lively during the depression years, to teach controversial subjects have been viewed with considerable suspicion and in some school systems have led to the scrutiny and withdrawal of textbooks, especially in the social studies, and even on one occasion to the burning of one well-known series. Nor have textbooks in history been immune from attacks, censorship, or rejection as presenting what were regarded as unfavorable or subversive interpretations of men and subjects. It may be expected, however, that, as Americans learn to live with the dangers that have followed World War II and at the same time to hold fast to their traditional freedoms, captious or intolerant criticism of the schools will decline and that the public will rely on its educational leaders for guidance rather than on groups which are themselves strongly partisan and self-interested. The leaders, however, will have to show less resentment at criticisms leveled against the public schools and less complacency about the success of their operation. Not all critics are open to the charge that they are enemies of the public-school system. The leaders have a responsibility to the public, who maintain and support the schools, to sift the criticisms and distinguish between those that are justified and those that come from sources open to suspicion.

CHAPTER III

Education of the Child

THE CHANGING CHARACTER OF EDUCATION

No part of the American educational system has been so much exposed to the play of conflicting theories as the education of the child. Even more than the education of the adolescent, or secondary education which has its own plethora of controversial issues, elementary education has been subjected to a variety of theories regarding aims, content, and methods of instruction. It would be necessary to go back at least sixty years, to the last decade of the nineteenth century, to trace the development of the controversies that have had the education of the child from the kindergarten through the elementary school as their center. The turning point in the history of elementary education may be placed at about 1890. This does not mean that changes took place as soon as they were suggested by the theorists, but that a more clearly pronounced American approach began to be evolved at about that date. The influence of the elementary-school tradition, with its emphasis on teaching the three R's, and the influence of foreign theories of education did not disappear at once: indeed, one theory developed by a German philosopher was brought back by enthusiastic American students, who had studied in Germany, and elaborated it in the United States over a period of years before it lost its vogue and yielded to new and more native influences.

The progress of elementary education, including the education of young children, was affected by other influences than the professional. The conquest of the frontier, the changes in the distribution of population, the increase in the flow of immigrants, the new industrial development and the rise of cities, and the new sense of nationalism, engendered by the Spanish-American War, and later the position of international leadership that followed the two World Wars were all factors that have called for an improvement in education generally. In the education of the child these factors emphasized necessary aspects of a foundation for membership in a democracy, the ideals of which this country undertook to disseminate through the world and of which it sought to serve as a model. With the improvement of the country's economic conditions and its increasing wealth, it became possible to raise and to enforce the requirements for school attendance, although it was not until 1918 that compulsory attendance to fourteen was enacted in Mississippi. The average length of term rose from 144.6 days in 1890 to 178.6 days in 1949–50. The physical plant of the school was gradually improved in safety, function, and appearance, and to the amenities of the buildings were added a wealth and variety of equipment. The slow development on the material side continued through the first half of this century.

The material improvements and advances, to which there were later added the latest devices for ventilation and lighting of schools and the provision of audio-visual aids, were secured through the efforts of a new body of school administrators, trained in the arts of public relations, and since these evidences of progress were visible and tangible and lent a new status to the school in its community, the public was ready in most cases to foot the bills. The advances of the teaching profession were much slower and, so far as elementary schools were concerned, neither salaries nor status were sufficient to keep men in the profession. Moreover, public habituated to thinking of elementary education as synonymous with instruction in the three R's could not understand or keep up with the evolution in the functions of the teacher and the school in relation to the children — Changes brought about by the newly developing and detailed scientific study of education and a new philosophical approach to the whole of education.

Sentiment for what was considered to be the traditional function of the elementary school persisted despite the almost sensational claims made for the new "progressive" theories of education and their practices in experimental schools. In the end, which came after World War II, the public or the vociferous part of it rose in revolt against "Progressive" education in the public schools on the ground of subversive teaching, a charge which was never substantiated, instead of being concerned about the unsatisfactory quality of the education given, for which some evidence might have been found.

At the same time that the revolt against the public schools, motivated by a variety of causes, took place, teachers began to leave the profession in large numbers attracted by more remunerative and perhaps less onerous jobs during and after World War II but also discouraged by the economic and other status allotted to them by the public and by school administrations. The exodus of teachers was serious in itself. For some years it added to the difficulty of recruiting candidates to be prepared for teaching. The serious shortage of teachers, moreover, coincided with an unanticipated increase in school enrollments that followed the increased birth rate during and after World War II. The shortage of teachers and the increased enrollments were accompanied by a shortage of school buildings and classrooms, a shortage due to the building restrictions during the war and in many localities to the migration of population in the wake of migrating industries. Large classes and double shifts were the inevitable consequences of these shortages. A normal situation is not to be expected for some years.

While these developments were proceeding, controversies were going on about every aspect of education, expecially at the elementary level. There was uncertainty about the content and the methods of instruction. There were those who were critical of the traditional emphasis on information, facts, and knowledge, and were more concerned with training pupils to learn for themselves than with teaching or "telling" them anything; in the opinion of this group pupils must not be taught "what" to think but "how" to think. This position brought to the fore a number of conflicts such as the place of freedom and discipline, of authority and self-expression, of acquisition of knowledge and self-realization, of pupil experience and adult expectations. At the heart of the controversies was the conflict between the child and the curriculum, and the fear that originality and creativity would be repressed by setting out something to be learned by the pupil. The traditional school, it was argued, had stood for "passive" learning; the pupil repeated, memorized, and learned by rote material which he often did not understand, but the acquisition of which was claimed to be good for the training of his mind. The modern school emphasized activity and purpose motivating such activity and intellectual growth through acquiring ability to meet new situations and solving problems; content, it is claimed, is acquired incidentally and its meaning is understood because it is acquired for a purpose. Following this theory the time-table of the traditional school disappears and the curriculum, instead of being fragmented into separate subjects, consists of integrated or interdisciplinary blocs of studies with different subjects being drawn upon as the need for them arises. Discipline and order it was argued would take care of themselves because pupils would devote their efforts wholeheartedly to carrying out their purpose.

REORGANIZATION OF THE SYSTEM

Not only has the pattern of the education of children been changed since the beginning of the century, but important modifications have been made in its organization. The traditional system of elementary schools was developed during the nineteenth century, consisting generally of eight grades for children from the age of six to the age of fourteen. The kindergarten for younger children below the age of six had been introduced in this country by Mrs. Carl Schurz in 1856 and it was developed mainly as a private institution, although after its adoption in St. Louis in 1873 through the efforts of William Torrey Harris it found its way very slowly into the public-school system. The nursery school for children from about the ages of two to four or five was developed much later and did not become recognized as important for the growth of the child until after World War I.

At the other end of elementary education came the high school which offered a four-year course. It was recognized in the last decade of the nineteenth century that the length of the course was inadequate for the purpose of a sound secondary education as then conceived and that the transition from the elementary to the high school was too abrupt for most pupils because of the differences in content, methods of instruction, and methods of work. It was proposed by the Committee of Ten of the National Education Association, in its report of 1893, that a six-year course of secondary education would be more appropriate to overcome these two weaknesses of the organization. The Committee of Fifteen of the same association, reporting on elementary education in 1895, was opposed to reducing the length of the elementary course but agreed that it was desirable to improve the articulation with the high schools. It was not until about 1910 that the movement began to spread to establish the junior high school which included the last two years of the elementary and the first year of the high school. In systems which did not adopt the junior high school, the last two years — the seventh and eighth grades — of the elementary school began to be treated as an intermediate unit intended to bridge the transition from the primary to the secondary stages of education and to give pupils guidance for their high-school studies.

A similar problem of articulation presented itself at the other end of the elementary school. The transition from the kindergarten of the traditional Froebelian type to the first grade of the elementary school was even more abrupt than from the eighth grade to the first year of the high school. Nor in view of the more serious differences in philosophy dominating the two stages of education was it possible to make any adjustments until the time came when the character of the kindergarten was changed and that of the early grades of the elementary school began slowly to be modified. In the end, as will appear later, it was the reformed doctrine of the kindergarten that was to bring about a reform in the early grades and a new unit, known as the "primary unit," emerged to which the nursery-school principles also contributed.

The establishment of the first kindergarten by private and philanthropic agencies preceded the nursery schools by nearly seventy-five years. Kindergartens began to be established as parts of the public school systems between 1880 and 1900, but it was many years before their inclusion in such systems was sanctioned in practically all state education laws. The reason for the lack of appeal was due to the domination of their practices by the philosophy of their originator, Fredrich Froebel, which Americans regarded as too mystical. The characteristic arrangement of the classroom — the circle, the "gifts" and occupations, the games and plays, combined into a Uniform Program which did not permit of any deviation — was felt to be too rigid. The symbolism of the gifts — cubes, spheres, and cylinders — whereby unity with the divine was to be promoted had no appeal for American parents and little meaning for the public.

The revolt began in 1890 and was led by Anna Bryan and Patty Smith Hill, the latter of whom was to become professor of education at Teachers College and a recognized leader in the reform of early childhood education. The two critics of the Froebelian system rebelled against its rigidity and symbolism, and under the influence of the new child-study movements looked for and developed new games, plays, songs, stories, and activities better adapted to children's interests and the needs for their growth. There arose two camps which persisted until 1913 when, to the distress of the conservative Froebelians, the progressives under the leadership of Patty S. Hill carried the day. In the same year the unification of the kindergarten and primary grades was begun at the University of Chicago.

The beginnings of the reform movement coincided with the beginnings of a rapidly developed child-study movement, inspired by the achievements of psychological research in Germany and in this country. In 1888 the Society for the Study of Child Nature was founded; in 1908 the Federation of Child Study was organized and later became the Child Study Association of America. In 1912 the Children's Bureau was established in the Department of Labor to look after the welfare and interests of children. In 1911 the Yale Psychological Clinic was created, followed in 1917 by the Iowa Child Welfare Research Station, both dedicated to scientific research into the problem of child growth and development. Centers for research in child welfare were established at Teachers College, Columbia University, the University of Minnesota, University of Iowa, University of California, and Yale University through grants from the Laura Spelman Rockefeller Memorial. All the centers devoted their attention mainly to the study of the preschool child. The importance attached to this movement was manifested by the proceedings of the White House Conference on Child Health and Protection (1930). These developments coincided with the interest that began to be shown in the nursery school and helped to promote that interest by emphasizing the importance of the early years of childhood for physical and mental growth. It was as a result of these activities that the term "preschool" came to be considered a misnomer, because it seemed to differentiate too much between the child's development before and after entering school. The continuity of the child's growth and development was emphasized and the activities and experiences provided for the child were differentiated according to its maturity. The distinction between the preschool and school proper was eliminated by the organization of the early years of schooling into a "primary unit."

The principles that determined the change in the character of the kindergarten have already been mentioned. They represented a more realistic approach to the interests and needs of the child than the formal, symbolic philosophy of Froebel (or, later, the formal and stereotyped apparatus developed by Maria Montessori). The modern kindergarten places its emphasis on the development of good habits, training in coöperation with others, physical progress through a variety of activities suited to the children's stage of growth, and mental progress through a variety of experiences — play, story-telling, music, rhythm, creative activities in art and manual work, and opportunities to develop a vocabulary and expression, which will promote a readiness for some of the more formal work of the grades.

From the point of view of organization kindergartens are either private and fee-paying or parts of the public-school system in increasing numbers since 1920. Generally the pupils are four or five years old, the lower age being more prevalent in the private than in public kindergartens. The latter, found more generally in city school systems and in consolidated rural schools, are beginning to be so over-crowded, that pupils attend either a morning or afternoon session. In 1949–50 the public kindergartens had an enroll-ment of 1,034,000 children out of the 19,405,000 pupils enrolled in elementary schools.

The kindergarten, like the nursery schools, has among its functions the task of serving as a center for the education of parents through conferences with the teachers and group meetings. If the early years of childhood are important for the growth and development of children, the education of parents to deal with the early years of this development is important and is facilitated by the fact, brought out at the White House Conference of 1930, that parents show greater interest in the care and protection of their children up to the age of six than at any other stage of their growth.

The last three decades have witnessed the further extension of provisions for the educational care of children younger than those for whom the kindergarten is intended. The kin-dergarten and nursery school may overlap in the last two years, but the latter may admit children at the age of two and hold them until the age of six. The nursery schools must be distinguished from the day nurseries or crèches, established by philanthropic and other private agencies to look after the physical care of infants and children of working women. The nursery schools are a late development which had their origin in England when the McMillan sisters saw the need of providing for more than the physical care of the children of the underprivileged and of giving them an opportunity for healthy all-round growth under conditions similar to those enjoyed by children of the privileged in their nurseries. In the United States the nursery schools were originally adopted as centers for psychological research into the physi-cal and mental development of children. Such centers were usually attached to institutions mentioned earlier as created for the study of children. They were also established in connection with high schools and colleges to train students in the care of children. Their further development came as a result of the declining size of families and the necessity of providing companionship for the lone child; their usefulness was also recognized as the number of women who continued their careers after marriage increased.

The largest development of nursery schools occurred during the depression years of the 'thirties when the Federal government undertook to provide subsidies for their establishment and maintenance to meet the emergency situation that was likely to affect children detrimentally on account of the unemployment and insecurity of their parents. Funds were provided to the states and localities first through the Federal Emergency Relief Authority, then the Works Progress Administration, and finally the Federal Works Administration.

With the urgent demand for manpower and the employment of women in war industries and other activities during World War II attention was sharply drawn to the need for the care of young children. Funds were provided by the federal government through the Lanham Act and by several state legislatures (California, Connecticut, New York, Pennsylvania, and Washington) for the establishment of wartime nursery schools and child-care centers. The Federal grants were discontinued in 1946, but the nursery-school idea was now established on a firm footing and was provided as an integral part of some public-school systems or of private experimental schools and as private ventures. Because of the indifferent character of the last type at least one state, New York, in 1939 required private nursery schools to be registered.

The nursery school in many respects follows the same principles that now rule the kindergarten, allowing for differences in the ages of the children. The nursery school has a greater responsibility for the training of the young pupils in physical habits; for that reason the size of the group under one teacher is generally limited to fifteen. Because the children stay in the nursery school for a longer day than they do in the kindergarten, provision is made for meals and rest periods. Otherwise the activities are like those in the kindergarten and consist of play in groups, training in healthful living and hygienic habits, music and rhythm, dance, dramatization, drawing and painting, and work with clay and wood. Activities are conducted indoors and outdoors, and opportunities are created for the development of speed and expression. The aim in general is to cultivate a happier and healthier childhood.

Parents are expected, and indeed the age of the children compels them, until school-going has become a habit, to take an even more direct interest in the work of the nursery school than of the kindergarten. Not only do they have conferences with the teachers but they often spend a considerable amount of time in the schools, partly to help the teachers and partly to ensure security for the child in its first venture away from home. Psychologists claim that the growth of children at the nursery school and kindergarten stage is greater in scope and extent than at any other stage of their development, since they are not only discovering but creating a new world for themselves. So far as the effects of attendance at kindergartens are concerned, investigations have reported that the number of repeaters in the grades is smaller among children who have attended kindergartens than among those who have not. This point, however, is not nearly as important as the emphasis in both nursery schools and kindergartens on healthful growth of children and the guidance given to parents who may need it.

It is perhaps not without significance that neither nursery schools nor kindergartens were subjected to the criticisms leveled against education in general after World War II. The explanation is perhaps to be found in the fact that they presented a new pattern of education of which not many adults had had any experience and, therefore, no standard of reference or expectations derived from their own school days. Furthermore, the kindergartens and nursery schools were definitely directed to giving young children the kind of education or opportunities for development that any good home would seek to give. Nor has there been as much vacillation about the aims, content, and method in early childhood education as has been characteristic in the past half century of both elementary an secondary education.

CHANGING CHARACTER OF THE ELEMENTARY SCHOOL

In presenting an account of the history of elementary education in the past fifty years it is difficult to make any generalizations. This difficulty is due to a number of reasons, caused by the size of country with its lack of uniformity and by the rapid changes from an agricultural to a predominantly industrial economy with its varied demands for manpower. The changing character and flow of immigration at the end of the nineteenth and beginning of the twentieth centuries intensified the difficulties that the school had to meet. The Americanization of the immigrants, speaking different languages and coming from different backgrounds of culture patterns, was, indeed, recognized as one of the important tasks of education, and of elementary education in particular. How well that task has been performed was amply demonstrated in the two World Wars as well as by the cultural contributions of the immigrants to the country of their adoption. Writing in 1931 a German educator testified to the success of the schools in Americanizing the foreigner. "The success of the school," he wrote, "is seen when one observes with astonishment and often with sorrow how often the immigrant from the most diverse parts of Europe are absorbed and transformed into Americans. Some schools publish the

names and photographs of graduating students in their Yearbooks; the names and given names may be German or perhaps
Italian and the appearance already slightly Americanized —
but they are fully American in thought and feeling." [1]

More than these causes that make generalization difficult
is the fact noted in 1901 by Sir Joshua Fitch, an English
educator, as a characteristic of American education: "America may be regarded as a laboratory in which educational
experiments are being tried out on a great scale under conditions exceptionally favorable to the encouragement of inventiveness and fresh enthusiasm, and to the discovery of
new methods and new truths." Experimentation has kept education, elementary education in particular, in a state of fer-
ment since at least 1890 and at an increasing rate since World
War I. It is easy enough to trace changes in theory but more
difficult to discover the extent to which the schools responded
to these changes. There is evidence that teachers tend to
become habituated to routine practices. The criticisms of
education since World War II would, however, indicate that
changes of emphasis have found their way into some school
systems.

The character of elementary education began to change
before 1890 as, for example, through the influence of Edward
A. Sheldon who, as superintendent of schools and principal
of the normal school in Oswego, New York (1853–97),
reorganized the curriculum and methods of the elementary
schools largely on the model of the English Home and
Colonial Infant Society's adaptation of the doctrines of Pestalozzi. The chief feature of the Oswego Movement was its
emphasis on object teaching and nature study, on the basis
of which William Torrey Harris, as superintendent of schools
in St. Louis (1866–80), worked out a program of elementary
science. Others developed other subjects of the elementary
school curriculum and contributed to its enrichment. The
most notable of the early reformers was Colonel Francis W.

Parker, whose main contributions were the improvement of the teaching of geography (1889) and an experiment on the concentration of subjects. The practices of the elementary school were widely questioned, and among those who stimulated inquiry was President Charles W. Eliot of Harvard University, whose papers when read at meetings of the National Education Association stirred up widespread discussion not only of the elementary school curriculum, but also of the organization of the educational system in general.

THE PSYCHOLOGICAL BASES OF REFORM

The movements for reform were empirical and intuitive. There was as yet no systematic basis either in psychology or in philosophy of education to serve as a guide for advance. The study of education as a social process or as a science had not yet begun. In the last decade of the nineteenth century considerable advance had been made to correct these deficiencies. Pestalozzi, of course, had made the psychologizing of education the central aim of his doctrine, and Froebel after him had directed attention to the need of understanding children at their stage of development, but neither possessed more than a superficial understanding of psychology. The subject began to be modernized and placed on a scientific foundation of accuracy and objectivity instead of remaining the branch of metaphysics it was. Wilhelm Wundt in 1879 opened in Leipzig a laboratory for the experimental study of psychology. The philosophical foundations of education came from two directions — one foreign and the other American. The former was the philosophy of Johann Friedrich Herbart and the latter of John Dewey. Herbartian influence helped to revitalize methods of instruction in particular as well as to give new point to content for about two decades. Dewey's philosophy led to a complete reconstruction in education which, beginning about 1915 in private experimental schools, has persisted through various interpretations to the present.

Among Wundt's students in Leipzig were two Americans, who were to contribute to the redirection of psychology in the United States. Of these G. Stanley Hall established a laboratory for experimental psychology at Johns Hopkins University in 1883 and later made Clark University, of which he became president, a center for psychological research. Hall may have been influenced in his work as much by Wilhelm Preyer who published *Die Seele des Kindes* in 1882 (*The Mind of the Child*, 1890) as by Wundt and contributed considerably to the launching of the child study movement and to the more scientific movement of research into the original nature of the child. A follower of Herbart, he was associated with a group that held the culture-epoch theory, and believed that the child in its development recapitulated the stages of the cultural development of the race. While this theory was discarded later, Hall undoubtedly promoted the genetic approach in psychology. His most important contribution, however, was his massive two volume study, *Adolescence, Its Psychology and Its Relation to Physiology, Anthropology, Sociology, Sex, Crime, Religion, and Education* (New York, 1904). The study, which was fundamental and exercised considerable influence on the progress of secondary education for many years, has been superseded by later research which it helped to inspire. To elementary education Hall's disciples made many contributions, particularly through their researches in the field of child study.

The second American student of Wundt was J. McKeen Cattell who established a psychological laboratory at Columbia University and was the first to promote the statistical study of heredity and the original nature of man, following the lines of research begun earlier in England by Francis Galton and Karl Pearson. Another landmark in the development of the scientific study of psychology which laid the foundations for modern movements in education was the work of William James of Harvard University. In 1890

James published his *Principles of Psychology*, and in 1899, *Talks on Psychology of Interest to Teachers*, a series of lectures delivered in 1891. His work represented on the one side an all-round attack on the prevalent faculty psychology, and on the other dealt with questions of child development which were of direct interest to the classroom teacher.

The work of those three pioneers coalesced in the work of Edward L. Thorndike, who had been a student of William James at Harvard and of J. McKeen Cattell at Columbia. His contributions and researches covered the whole range of the human being from infancy to old age. Thorndike not only contributed to a better understanding of original nature and nurture, of heredity and environment, based on biological and materialistic principles instead of a priori speculation. His three-volume *Educational Psychology*, begun in 1903 and completed in 1913, exercised a profound influence on the development of educational psychology. His treatment was comprehensive and the second volume of his *Educational Psychology*, devoted to the *Psychology of the Laws of Learning* which also introduced a new interpretation of interest, affected the practice of education and was used to support the activity movement almost immediately. Equally influential was his contribution to the knowledge of individual differences which in turn was to become the rationale for individualized instruction. Thorndike's name will always be associated with two other important contributions. James had helped to undermine the traditional faculty psychology and throw doubt on the doctrine of formal discipline and transfer, that is, the notion that the mind can be trained through the study of difficult and even unintelligible material and, when so trained, acquires the ability to deal with new material or situations. It was maintained that certain subjects were better for such training than others. The doctrine is as old as education. What James started was carried a stage further by Thorndike and others at the beginning of the century. Although it was claimed that the doctrine of formal discipline and transfer of training was "exploded" by these investigations, Thorndike made no such claim but insisted that "The real question is not. 'Does improvement of one function alter others? ' but, 'To what extent, and how, does it? ' " A third aspect of Thorndike's work was his contribution to mental measurements and the development of scales and tests of achievement which helped to define norms of standards of school work. Neither the idea of mental measurements nor of scales originated with Thorndike but he was able to bring to them the refinements of statistical methods which he had developed. In 1910 he published his handwriting scale, which followed by two years an arithmetic scale elaborated by one of his students and preceded many others until today there is scarcely any aspect of school work for which tests are not available.

Thorndike's work at Teachers College, Columbia University, was paralleled by the work of his contemporaries, Charles H. Judd at the University of Chicago, and Lewis M. Terman of Stanford University. The students of these three leaders in turn continued studies and research along the same lines in education departments and teachers colleges of other universities or as directors of research in public school systems and other agencies.

Thorndike's basic psychological theory was associationist or connectionist, as expressed in the stimulus-response (S-R) bond doctrine. This theory has been criticized but not wholly with justification. It was not until 1933, however, that Thorndike further explained the theory by bringing in the idea of belongingness which implied not direct response to a stimulus, as seemed to be implied in the connectionist principle, but selectivity and choice of response. Nevertheless, it was because of the idea of selectivity that *Gestalt* psychology attacked the theory of associationism and the laws of learning based on the theory. *Gestalt* psychology developed first in

Germany about 1912 and was brought to the attention of American students in a translation of Kurt Koffka's *The Growth of the Mind* in 1924 and later by the work of Kurt Lewin, a German psychologist who settled in this country. The basic principle of *Gestalt* psychology is that all mental phenomena are not made up of parts into which they can be analyzed but have a dynamic interdependence or configuration. A situation is recognized not by putting together its constituent parts but as a whole which is grasped as a result of 'insight' or ability to see relations rather than by means of analysis and synthesis. *Gestalt* psychology exercised an influence on the teaching of some subjects or confirmed older methods empirically derived, such as reading and spelling. It was also invoked by some educators to support the theory that in the learning and educative process "the whole child" is involved, although the theory itself had its origin in other sources.

The further development of educational psychology which seriously influenced educational practice followed the emphasis on the importance of recognizing individual differences, on the one hand, and the expansion of the concept of education to a conviction that an education concerned only with the accumulation of facts and information, an intellectualistic education, was incomplete since it neglected the equally important maturing of the emotions. A combination of these two approaches to education led to further and more detailed study of the emotions. Their effects on learning and general development directed attention to the importance of guidance of the individual pupil on the basis of all the information that can be obtained about him, and to the meaning and development of personality. A further outgrowth of this trend was the study of the pupil's cultural, social, and economic background and its effects upon him, a point of approach also suggested by the study of educational sociology, concerned with the influence of culture patterns on education in general and on the individual. Since the end of education is held to be the development of the individual as a member of society, the emphasis on personality is also concerned with his attitudes, ideals, and conduct. Finally, although resisted for a long time, the influence of psychoanalysis could not be evaded, and, since guidance had already become a matter of concern to educators and educational psychologists, the problem of adjustment and maladjustment and their causes had to be investigated. In the little more than half a century the problems of education which were dealt with in books on school management, such as discipline, interest, and methods of teaching, have expanded to such a degree that what was at one time a single specialty has ramified into innumerable specialties, each concerned with some particular phase of the educational and instructional process.

RESEARCH IN EDUCATION

In the last years of the nineteenth century the questions whether education is an art or a science and whether there can be such a field as a science of education were widely discussed in the United States as well as in Great Britain and Germany. Professor Josiah Royce stated positively in 1891 that teaching is an art and that there is no science of education. "But, on the other hand," he went on, "if the teacher wants aid from the scientific spirit, and counsel from scientific education, there stands ready to his hand such assistance, as above all, psychology has to offer to the educator who desires to become a living observer of the minds of children, and such assistance, too, as ethics may suggest to the man who is strong enough to grapple with deeper problems." In 1891 education as a study depended upon borrowing from other fields such as philosophy, ethics, psychology, physiology, and logic. As will appear in ChapterV, the next thirty years saw not only the study of education established in its own right but the emergence and expansion of the scientific study of education as a branch of it. There have been times, indeed, when the specialists in the field of educational science have claimed that their science could determine the aims and purposes of education. This point of view has been rejected and a dominant place has been retained for a philosophy of education, while the actual task of teaching is still recognized to be an art, to the application of which the science of education can contribute.

It is doubtful whether the pioneers in child study, educational psychology, and tests and measurements could have anticipated the scope and range of the areas of research that have grown out of their pioneer studies. The progress of the sciences has undoubtedly served as a stimulus to research in other areas of human activities, when everything from advertising to the atom has become a subject of research and when the magic words, "research has proved," are enough to carry conviction and dissipate doubts. In the problems of education, research was not possible until instruments and techniques of objective investigation were made available, as they began to be early in the present century. The extent of the research productions has been phenomenal. While much has been superficial through inadequate training in the methods, particularly those based on mathematics, or unimportant and trifling because the problems were not worth studying, valuable contributions of a statistical nature have been made. The search for incontrovertible laws on which education and instruction could be based has not been and probably will never be successful and the hope of developing a science of "human engineering" is fortunately unrealizable.

The first ten or fifteen years of the century were devoted, first, to elaborating the instruments and methods of research and experimentation, and, second, to securing the interest and support of the profession. It was not easy to secure acceptance of the idea that most of the activities in education were capable of measurement. World War I and the necessity for selecting and classifying manpower for the Armed Forces provided the opportunity for the nationwide use of intelligence and other tests on a sufficiently large scale to carry conviction. Success hastened the expansion of research in all directions where comparable measures were needed.

The measures had already been applied to the study of school systems which had begun in 1911. These surveys, which took the place of assessment by the officials of governments in other countries, were invited by school authorities to investigate their schools, evaluate the results in the light of standards in other school systems, and offer suggestions for improvements considered desirable. Valuable as these surveys were in judging the status and standards of a school system, perhaps the most useful result was the creation of local bureaus of research to maintain continuous surveys in matters both of education and instruction and of organization and administration. To this end objective measures and standards constitute important instruments. By 1915 there were enough such bureaus for the experts to organize the National Association of Directors of Research which in 1922 became the American Educational Research Association. This Association in 1936 sponsored the preparation of the *Encyclopedia of Educational Research*, which was published in 1941 and in a revised edition in 1951 under the editorship of Walter S. Monroe of the University of Illinois. The 1520 double-column pages of the volume constitute a mine of information and references on every aspect of research in matters that have any bearing at all on education.

University departments of education and teachers colleges established their own research bureaus to serve their own areas of influence and to train experts for the field. "Investigation of educational foundations" was recognized as a function of such departments by Dean James E. Russell of Teachers College, Columbia University, as early as 1900. In 1922 the National Education Association created its own research bureau which is concerned with the collection and dissemination of information on education rather than experimentation or measurement. Throughout the country a similar function is also performed by the research bureau of the United States Office of Education. To these must be added the promotion of research by the National Society for the Study of Education which for several decades has devoted its Yearbooks to the study of some special aspect of education. Still later the many specialist organizations of professors of education, administrators, principals, supervisors, and classroom teachers have also issued Yearbooks devoted to research or reports in their own areas of interest.

In 1948 a number of educational research organizations were brought together with the financial assistance of the Carnegie Corporation to form the Educational Testing Service, located in Princeton, N. J. The organizations included in the group are the College Entrance Examination Board, the American Council on Education Psychological Examination, The Cooperative Test Service, the National Teacher Examinations, and the Graduate Records Examination.

The research developments of the objective type have been of undoubted service not only in education but also for classification and selection for the Armed Forces in two World Wars. They have also served a purpose in business and industry. At times, however, their value has been exaggerated. The faith, which was built up in the early years of its development, in the intelligence quotient (I.Q.), has been shaken by evidence that the measure is not constant. While achievement tests seem to be more reliable, there is some fear that the norms may have led to uniformity and standardization, on the one hand, and that, on the other, they may have been misused to establish standards to be reached rather than as methods for discovering weaknesses either in the pupil or in the teacher's methods. Rightly or wrongly there has taken place in recent educational theory a revolt against standards on the ground that each pupil is unique and that any measures of growth or development should be in terms of his own ability and personality rather than of the standards of a group.

Before the scientific study by the use of objective, statistical methods established itself elementary education came under the influence of a group of American educators who had studied in Germany and returned to disseminate the educational philosophy of Johann Friedrich Herbart and the school practices of the Herbartians. This influence lasted until its dominance was challenged by the advance in educational psychology, the results of research, and a new philosophy of education. Herbartianism continued to be prominent on the educational scene for a generation after the return about 1890 to this country of the American educators who helped to revitalize elementary education and to improve the preparation of teachers. The poor general and professional training of elementary school teachers had consisted of brief preparation in elementary school subjects and methods of school management on top of little more than an uncompleted high school education. To compensate for the inadequate preparation, the work of the teachers was conducted with the help of courses of study prescribed in detail, textbooks written more from the point of view of adults than of children, supervision to see that teachers followed instructions as prescribed, and examinations which were as much tests of the ability of the teachers as of their pupils. The method of instruction that had emerged out of this arrangement was the "recitation method," which encouraged memorization and rote learning of material assigned in textbooks and "reciting" the answers in class. The justification of the method, if the question was raised, was that the study of a varied collection of facts and information, even though their meaning was not comprehended, trained the different faculties of the mind and the mind so trained could successfully attack new material and problems. Faculty psychology and the doctrine of formal discipline continued to persist for many years after psychologists had shown that they were not sound or valid.

To this scene the Herbartians brought a new psychological concept of the mind operating as a whole, a new interest in the pupils stemming from the early child-study movement, a new approach to the curriculum, and a new method of instruction. Reference has already been made to the work of Colonel Francis W. Parker, who attracted the attention of educators to his innovations, first in Quincy, Mass., to break down the practice of mass instruction and neglect of individual differences, and then in Cook County (Illinois) Normal School, where he engaged in the reform of the elementary-school curriculum and endeavored, by concentrating a number of subjects around geography, to reduce the fragmentation of the curriculum into a multiplicity of separate subjects, and to promote a better understanding of child nature in methods of instruction.

The educators most prominently associated with the introduction and development of Herbartian philosophy in this country were Charles DeGarmo, Charles A. and Frank M. McMurry, and C. C. VanLiew. In 1893 Charles McMurry organized the Herbart Club (originally the Illinois School-masters Club), which in 1895, at a meeting of the National Education Association in Denver, became the National Herbart Society for the Scientific Study of Education. The Society included the names of Nicholas Murray Butler, Elmer E. Brown, Levi Seeley as well as those mentioned as the leaders of the movement. The purpose of the Society was declared to be "to study and investigate and discuss important problems of education. Its members do not subscribe to the doctrines of any one leader but seek for fair and thorough discussion." In 1902 following a serious criticism by Professor John Dewey of the Herbartian doctrine of interest, the name of

Herbart was dropped from the title of the Society. The National Society for the Study of Education was dedicated to "the serious, continuous, and intensive study of educational problems" without standing for any particular creed or propaganda; in aim and spirit the Society sought to be scientific.

The Herbartians succeeded in imparting a new vitality to elementary education. They defined more clearly the aim of education and sought by their methods of instruction and the selection of content to show how intellectual training was related to character formation. They placed the child in the forefront of the educative process in the sense that they sought to psychologize the presentation of the content instead of imparting it in its logical organization. As early as 1895 this was recognized by the Committee of Fifteen of the National Education Association, when it stressed the importance of the study of children in a course for the training of teachers. "Modern education," wrote the Committee, "emphasizes the opinion that the child, not the subject of study, is the guide to the teacher's efforts. To know the child is of paramount importance. How to know the child must be an important item of instruction to the teacher in training. The child must be studied as to his physical, mental and moral condition." [2]

They introduced a new concept of interest as the starting point of a new methodology of teaching and learning. By developing what they then regarded as a proper and correct understanding of the operations of the mind, and by showing how through apperception ideas come to reach out for and become associated with other ideas, they aimed to demonstrate that education need not consist of fragments and discrete pieces of knowledge. They displaced faculty psychology, and secured widespread acceptance of the Herbartian general methods, which became known throughout the country as the "Five Formal Steps." As developed by Herbart's disciples in Germany and disseminated in the United States the Five Formal Steps consisted of preparation, presentation, association,

generalization, and application. Each lesson was expected to
be a unit organized according to this general method and so
arranged, if well worked out, that the end of each lesson served
as a preparation or incentive for the next step. On the organization of the curriculum they tended at first to adopt the culture epoch theory, or the principle that the educative process
is evolutionary and the child recapitulates the development of
the experiences of the race from primitive life to modern society. Although the interest of young children can only be in
the simpler, primitive activities, the Herbartians in the later
development of the curriculum of the elementary schools
made important contributions to developing each subject in
such a way as to make it interesting to the pupils and to encourage them to continue from one stage of interest to another.

Not the least important of these contributions was the movement to rid the curriculum of much useless and meaningless
information and to find a center or core around which a number of subjects or topics could be unified. Through the method of concentration the interconnectedness of knowledge
could be conveyed and training provided in drawing upon
various subjects for the solution of a problem. In this way the
material to be used would have more meaning and relevance
to the pupil. The advocates of the culture epoch theory found
an opportunity to study literature, art, and science in their historical development. The most popular subject for concentration was geography, because the subject could be treated
from both the scientific and humanistic sides.

Another group of educators of the Herbartian school sought
to break down the treatment of subjects in isolation by the
method of correlation. The Committee of Fifteen of the National Education Association in its report, published in 1895,
had already advocated the correlation of studies. By correlation the Committee understood "the selection and arrangement in an orderly sequence of such objects of study as shall

give the child an insight into the world that he lives in, and a command over its resources such as it obtained by a helpful coöperation with one's fellows. In a word the chief consideration to which all others are to be subordinated, in the opinion of your Committee, is this requirement of the civilization into which the child is born, as determining not only what he shall study in school, but what habits and customs he shall be taught in the family before school arrives. . ." [3]

By this method of correlation pupils could see the interrelation of disciplines and their bearing upon each other. Correlation also lent itself to helping pupils to see a subject's relevance to social life and its activities. Both concentrations and correlation were methods of organizing subjects and of instruction that called for intelligence, insight, and appreciation of meanings instead of mechanical and unintelligent memorization. What the pupil learned was not necessarily stored for later use, but its practical implications were brought out as part of the lesson.

Out of the methods of concentration and correlation, Professor Frank M. McMurry in particular developed the type study and topical lesson, in which a representative example or a general topic within the interest of the pupils would be taken up for comprehensive treatment. This involved the collection of relevant facts and information, concomitant elements to enlarge understanding of the topic, the formulation of an hypothesis or conclusion, verification, and systematization of what has been found, and the suggestion of another related problem. The methods could be employed in the study of history, geography, nature study, and composition. The value of the type study or topic as a point of concentration lay in giving the pupils an aim or goal for selecting the facts needed for the occasion and encouraged their own activity. The order of development of a topic was psychological rather than logical. The concluding task might call for logical arrangement.

Associated with these innovations, which were also incorporated in the organization of textbooks, was the emphasis on teaching pupils how to study. Like the type studies and topics, the process of study starts with a problem or difficulty to be overcome or solved or a need to be satisfied and involves the same steps as those described. The development of the method of study, embodied in a book on *How To Study and Teaching How To Study*, published in 1909, by Professor Frank M. McMurry, showed how the processes used in the school could be of use outside the school in meeting the ordinary contingencies of life. The activities which these methods encouraged pupils to undertake themselves rather than memorizing and reciting an assigned lesson were regarded as the important end to be achieved. "True or logical study is not aimless mental activity or passive reception of ideas only for the sake of having them. It is the vigorous application of the mind to a subject for the satisfaction of a felt need. Instead of being aimless, every portion of effort put forth is an organic step toward the accomplishment of a specific purpose; instead of being passive, it requires the reaction of the self upon the ideas presented, until they are supplemented, organized, and tentatively judged, so that they are held well in memory. The study of a subject has not reached its end until the guiding purpose has been accomplished and the knowledge so assimilated that it has been used in a normal way and has become experience." [4] The pupil rather than the teacher came to be regarded as the center of the educative process. The process did not relegate the teacher to the sidelines to advise when called upon as was to be the case later when the child-centered school emerged. The process was still under the control of the teacher; it was he who suggested the problems to be studied and helped to make them interesting and relevant to the pupils' stage of development. It was true that the interest advocated by the Herbartians was "extrinsic" but it was related in the minds of the teachers with something larger or more universal than the "intrinsic" interest that came from the pupils' own "felt needs," which became the slogan in subsequent developments.

THE INFLUENCE OF PRAGMATISM

In the end, however, the Herbartian philosophy was superseded, partly because the psychology on which it was based began to be proved unsound, and partly because the cult of the Five Formal Steps became more and more stilted, formalistic, and mechanical in the hands of teachers who preferred routine to considered preparation. Critics charged that greater attention was devoted to methods than to the curriculum, which may have been true in the work of the normal schools but not in the hands of some teachers who were artists. Although it was not wholly true that the Herbartians devoted little attention to the revision of the curriculum as a whole, the urge for the application of scientific methods to education which began about 1915 became widespread. The interest shifted from methods of instruction to a modernized version of Herbert Spencer's "What Knowledge Is Most Worth?" Educators began to search for that knowledge which society used most as shown in daily life and the printed pages of books, magazines, and newspapers. Arithmetic was reduced to "everyday arithmetic," science to "the science of everyday life"; history became a collection of the dates and events most frequently mentioned in printed matter; grammar was limited to such forms as occurred most frequently; word counts established the range of vocabulary to be prescribed for reading and spelling of pupils at the various stages of their education.

The movement to base the content of a subject on the material most frequently used was succeeded by a broader expansion of the aims of education and the content of the curriculum in general by what was then known as "job-analysis," the application to education of the methods used in industry by efficiency engineers. This approach to the curriculum was launched in 1909 by Professor W. W. Charters in his *Methods of Teaching Developed from a Functional Standpoint* and in 1913 in *Teaching the Common Branches*. The Committee on the Economy of Time, appointed by the National Education Association in 1911, recommended the use of scientific methods to determine the socially worthwhile instructional materials, the elimination of useless content, and adaptation to the life needs of the pupils. The Committee between 1915 and 1919 issued four Yearbooks through the National Society for the Study of Education.

Following this approach Professor Franklin Bobbitt in 1922 analyzed the activities of adult life and reduced some thousand objectives to ten divisions to serve as a guide to curriculum making. Professor Frederick G. Bonser in the same year grouped the major activities into four groups (health, fundamental processes, civic and social relations, and recreation). The selection of content to meet defined objectives followed these or similar lines and sought to combine the needs of adult life with methods adapted to the pupils' stages of maturity.

Curriculum reconstruction became one of the major activities in the years following World War I. Experts were invited by school systems either to undertake or to advise on the revision of the curriculum which had already been initiated by local groups of teachers. While the early years of the century were devoted mainly to perfecting methods of instruction, the decade from about 1911 on was devoted to the improvement of the curriculum. Both movements were inspired by the aim of making the educative process and its content more meaningful or functional for the pupils. In the first period efforts were devoted to making the work of the school interesting to the pupils and stimulating their self-activity. In the second period the content was revised so that the pupils could understand its meaning and purpose and its relation to the social life around them. The achievement of the pupils continued to be measured by tests which were themselves being continually revised. The time had not yet come when the acquisition of knowledge — "mere knowledge" as it was later referred to – was disparaged in favor of attitudes, ideals, behavior, and conduct. The aim was not to discard subject matter but to reorganize and revise the content from the point of view of social usefulness and to improve methods of instruction in the light of new psychology of the child and the learning process. In general greater activity of the pupils was favored instead of passive acquisition of information under the coercion of external discipline. In a word, the preoccupation of educators was more with methods of instruction designed to give greater stability to a carefully selected content rather than with a complete revolution of the educative process in terms of a theory based on the child's interests, his growth, and freedom, which was already being put into practice but chiefly in private experimental schools.

The new philosophy of education was rooted in the philosophy of pragmatism, which in itself represented a break with traditional philosophies and particularly with any philosophy which posited the existence of absolutes or permanent, unchanging ideals, or eternal verities. Pragmatism was essentially an American approach in philosophy and was first developed by Charles S. Pierce, who launched an attack on idealism in 1871, redefined knowledge and truth in terms of experience and experimentation, and insisted on the use of scientific method in all types of thinking. The concept was adopted by William James who refused, however, to recognize pragmatism as a philosophy; to him pragmatism never meant more than a method of conducting discussions. It was John Dewey who became the leading and most influential exponent of pragmatism both as a philosophy and as a method. He made pragmatism a revolutionary approach to education in his own laboratory school started in 1896 in Chicago "to train children in coöperation and mutually useful living." The practice and principles first developed there were then applied in a number of experimental and university laboratory schools. Ultimately but in modified form they found their way into public schools in different parts of the country. The influence of the new philosophy, however, extended predominantly to elementary schools only. Its leaders often deplored the fact that secondary education was not affected by the new theory, and it was not until almost the last decade of the half century that a few schools tried it in practice.

Inspired by the principles of Darwinian evolution and by the gradual emergence of scientific method, the philosophy of pragmatism is based on the assumption that the outstanding characteristic of life is change and that in a precarious world life must be in constant process of experimental adjustment to changing conditions. Since they are born of and refer back to the past, traditions and closed systems of absolutes, fixed principles, and abstractions must be discarded in favor of concreteness, facts, action, and power. In a constantly changing world, novel and problematic situations must be faced experimentally and by the methods used in science. Hence intelligence is not something that exists in advance but grows by being actively employed in meeting new situations and overcoming obstacles and difficulties that stand in the way of the smooth and ongoing process of life. From this general principle was derived the emphasis on knowledge, ideas, aims, ideals, and experience as active and valuable primarily not as stored-up possessions for future use, but as guides and instruments to be applied to solving problematic and novel situations that are met.

Only as new situations are faced experimentally rather than by the application of permanent standards or knowledge fixed-in-advance can obstructions be removed, problems be solved, and new truths be discovered. For truth is not something fixed and unchanging but something that is tested by the consequences of an action. What is found to work in meeting a difficulty or in solving a problem is true, but continues to be only a hypothesis subject to verification. No further validation of truth is needed than that the individual concerned in an action has found the consequences to be satisfactory in solving the difficulties and obstacles encountered. The individual, if he is to grow – and growth is the end of education — cannot accept the dictates of authority; he must be free to "think through" his own problems and arrive at a solution by his own thinking and the active use of his intelligence. Only as he is stimulated or motivated to activity by a purpose which arises from his own needs, purposes, or interests can the individual engage in an experience which is active and through which he can discover the knowledge, facts, and information necessary to carry out his purpose to a successful conclusion and be ready for further activity.

The function of the philosophy of education, the pragmatist maintained, is not to discover universals, extrinsic or absolute values, or eternal verities, which according to the theory are either nonexistent or authoritarian in character, and then proceed to incorporate these in curricula and courses of study to be learned by the pupils. The real task of a philosophy of education from the pragmatist's point of view is to define procedures by which the pupil will be placed in a position to develop his own values and to reconstruct his own experiences as the situation demands rather than to accept values and results of the experiences of others. Such a philosophy is concerned with the formulation of procedures for the development of right mental and moral attitudes. When properly developed such attitudes will cultivate in the pupil the ability to deal with concrete problems of immediate concern to him. The universe is indeterminate, precarious, and changing — "a universe with the lid off" — its characteristics are not fixity or certainty, but novelty, change, adaptation, adjustment, and growth.

The implication to be drawn from this position is that

thought and action are one and mutually interactive and that both are instruments to be applied to concrete events and situations. Education, according to the argument, has too long been concerned with the past which has no meaning except as it prepares for and is a stage toward the future. Intelligence, in the same way, is not something passive, ready to absorb knowledge like a sponge; it is creative and selective in deciding on the means and ends for action in meeting a situation. As the individual reconstructs his experience through the employment of scientific method, so the application of the scientific method to the material environment can produce a new civilization. In this way also there can be developed a closer relationship between cultural and spiritual life and the material environment from which it has always been separated in the past. The cultural lag which is the result of the persistence of traditional ideas and ideals will also be eliminated by this method. An essential characteristic of the pragmatic point of view is the effort to resolve the traditional dualisms such as the child and curriculum, school and society, interest and effort, thought and action, learning and doing; unification is to be found through interaction between the two poles. Ideas, ideals, knowledge, thinking, intelligence must not be allowed to be passive, but must be put to work in remaking the individual and society; in the process reconstruction and enrichment take place. The human organism, in other words, shows a readiness to react to stimuli and in the striving for equilibrium with its environment both the organism and the environment are affected in the process. Applied to education this means that the child learns through experience to control situations and develops as a social being by sharing in social experiences a coöperation with others.

Education from a pragmatic point of view is a process of development from within and not imposition from without. The process starts with the natural tendency of the child to be active and through active and direct participation either in problems or "felt needs" of his own or in social experiences with others reconstructs his experience in readiness for further development and growth. The process is made possible by the fact that the child is plastic and adaptable for growth which responds to the stimuli of the environment or experiences or shared interests. Growth, like education, comes from the continuous reorganizing and reconstruction of meanings, an intensive process which, according to its proponents, cannot be promoted by external pressure or imposition that places a premium on unquestioning conformity to a fixed and static environment and on docile acceptance of authority. The consequences of action alone serve to promote growth.

Growth is promoted when the equilibrium between the organism and the environment is disturbed or when obstacles are encountered to the ongoing process of thought or action. The organism grows when it has a "felt need" to solve a situation for which it must "contrive" the right responses and thereby acquire new meanings, attitudes, or dispositions to action. In such situations it is not knowledge fixed-in-advance but ability to employ the method of acquiring and using the appropriate knowledge that is desirable.

The educative process must, therefore, be centered in the pupils' own needs, interests, and purposes, which cannot be assigned or imposed by the teacher. Growth leading to further growth is only possible if the pupils' purposes are spontaneous and whole-hearted, and originate in his own felt needs when stimulated by a problematic situation. Activity then becomes purposeful and continues until the purpose is achieved satisfactorily. The assignment of purposes, predetermined objectives, subject matter fixed in advance or set out to be learned lead to docility, passive memorization, and rote learning, and conformity to things as they are without providing any opportunity for creativity, initiative, or originality. Activities in which the pupil engages because he has a purpose of his own help him to adapt himself to changing conditions and to develop a "dynamic" type of mind. Effort is put forth spontaneously without any pressure or discipline from without because the pupil has a genuine interest in achieving his purpose. It is not necessary under such conditions to make learning "interesting" by external devices. Whatever knowledge the pupil has is put to use, is instrumental, and is added to or reconstructed in the process of using it. The pupil "learns by doing," according to a widely repeated slogan, and he "lives what he learns." Education, according to another professionally popular phrase, is "life and not a preparation for life"; it is self-directing and self-disciplinary. Subject matter as such, curricula, and courses of study are abandoned in favor of "learning-situations" or activities which release creative intelligence and provide a succession of novelty developing situations or experiences.

As in mental activities, so in moral situations the pupil must be permitted to make his own choices and to create his own values in accordance with his own judgment of the consequences of his actions. Questions of conduct are not settled in advance and there can be no universal agreement about them, or about right or wrong apart from the situation concerned. The pupil must have the responsibility for working out his own code of conduct by seeing how it works. The authority of society or of any part of it should not be presented as a guide to conduct, or, as one writer says: "It is an immoral procedure for adults to seek to determine the future thought and conduct of a child." Reliance must be placed on the experience of each individual, on the use of the experimental method, and on critical examination by each of how his conduct works. The emphasis should be on the freedom of the child who should be permitted to grow in the light of his own experiences and activities and in the light of the consequences that ensue. This theory of character formation was expressed as follows in a yearbook of the Department of Superintendence:

It is unnecessary and undesirable, however, to pretend to the child that questions of conduct are all settled or that there is universal agreement upon them. Before his habits have become crystallized he should be introduced to this diversity and should be led to explore the facts and arguments bearing on debatable issues. . . The present trend in theory is to place on the child the responsibility of working out his own code of conduct with some help from the teachers and other adults in analyzing situations and with such light as he can get from a study of the history of mankind's experience with similar problems. . . The experience of the race in discovering what line of conduct works out satisfactorily and what does not is utilized only in so far as the child sees fit to appeal to it.[5]

According to the theory under discussion the social development of the child would be promoted and stimulated: first, because the activities engaged in would inevitably reflect the society around him; and, secondly, because the traditional practice encouraging competition in the classroom and success through effort would be abandoned in favor of social participation and coöperation in activities in which all pupils would take part. In one of his earliest contributions to education, *My Pedagogical Creed* (1897), Dewey expressed his belief that "the social life of the child is the basis of concentration, or correlation, in all his training or growth. The social life gives the unconscious unity and the background of all his efforts and of all his attainments. . . the true centre of correlation on the school subjects is not science, nor literature, not history, nor geography, but the child's own social activities." [6] In *Democracy and Education*, which appeared almost twenty years later, he wrote: "Moreover, the curriculum must be planned with reference to placing essentials first, and refinements second. The things which are socially most fundamental, that is, which have to do with the experiences in which the widest groups share, are the essentials." [7] The type of social life which is most desirable is the democratic since it is based on a recognition of the worth and dignity of the human being, provides multifarious opportunities for the promotion of mutual interests as a form of social control, and encourages interaction and coöperation between social groups. In an interview on the occasion of his eighty-fifth birthday Dewey summarized his fundamental principles as follows: "Society is in the process of undergoing great changes. It is essential that the schools readjust themselves so as to be able to give direction to these changes. Progressive education gave greater attention to the child's health and physical welfare. It is based on the identity of democratic government with self-government." [8]

Dewey's philosophy of education exercised the most profound influence on American education and in other countries where it merged with similar pedagogical trends that emphasized the right of the child to his own fullest development instead of being regarded as a plastic creature to be molded to an adult pattern. His earliest attack on educational theory was his discussion of *Interest as Related to Will* (later published as *Interest and Effort in Education*), in which he attacked the current concept of interest as something extrinsic, as sugar-coating to make lessons otherwise unpalatable or meaningless in the life of the child attractive and to call forth effort. From this he went on to attack the curriculum and its compartments of different subjects which might be justified logically but were not psychologically related to the child's intrinsic interests. Subjects were too abruptly introduced as special studies which broke up the essential unity of the child's life. The child should be encouraged to engage in all kinds of constructive activities and experiences which reproduce the activities of civilization and the world around him. He was opposed to the current proposals to find centers for concentration or correlation as put forward and tried by Colonel Francis W. Parker and the Herbartians. He stressed the importance for growth of activities which have meaning for the child, in which he has a spontaneous interest, and which he finds useful in the process of his education. The function of the teacher is to create situations that would enlist the child's efforts in meaningful and purposeful activities because they represent his own interests.

The aspects of Dewey's philosophy that attracted the most widespread interest were his respect for the child and his growth and the emphasis on activity. The protest against traditional practices which, it was charged, not only demanded but conduced pupils to passivity, docility, obedience, and rote learning, with the correlative strict discipline, had an important influence on the material side. The traditional classroom with its fixed forms and desks was designed for mass instruction and passive learning. It directed the attention of all the pupils to the teacher. The introduction of individual and moveable chairs and desks or tables can be attributed to the influence of Dewey's emphasis on activity and movement; the grouping and regrouping of the pupils in the classroom for their coöperative activities called for a change of furniture.

Concentration on the child, which came in part from the child study movement and child psychology, through the new philosophies of education (both Herbartianism and pragmatism), and a certain humanitarianism began to spread in social affairs toward the end of the nineteenth century, and directed attention to the child, at times somewhat sentimentally. Important as was this new attention devoted to one datum of education, the other datum — the materials and content of education — tended to be ignored or disparaged. There seemed to be a revolt against the traditional organization of the curriculum and course of study by subjects and a movement to replace them by purposeful activities, crystallized later into projects. Dewey's early statement in *My Pedagogical Creed* was forgotten that "the subject matter of the school curriculum should mark a gradual differentiation out of the primitive unconscious unity of social life." [9] Dewey took occasion in *Experience and Education* (1938), which was a critical examination of the trends in the new education, to remind the educational world of the need of logical organization of facts and ideas as an ideal in the educational process.[10] In the same year, Professor Boyd H. Bode maintained in *Progressive Education at the Crossroads* that traditional subjects had an educational value that could not be neglected without peril.[11]

By the time these criticisms were made the "child-centered" schools, which had sought in the 'twenties to put the pragmatic theory into practice, had run their course. They had concentrated their work on the needs and interests of children, had encouraged freedom and self-discipline without cultivating a sense of responsibility, and had emphasized the development of attitudes and dispositions and methods of "problem-solving" and "meeting situations" at the expense of imparting facts, information and respect for knowledge. "Mere" knowledge was subordinated to the cultivation of scientific method, research ability, and critical open-mindedness. The emphasis, it was claimed, was on teaching pupils "how to think" rather than "what to think," an emphasis inspired by the fear of "telling" pupils anything and of a policy of letting them look for and discover for themselves such information as they might need. Indoctrination and external discipline were regarded as imposition which made for docility and obedience to authority. There were enough examples of this misinterpretation of the ideas of freedom and authority to call for a rebuke from Dewey against the notion that an end or plan should not be suggested to the pupils because it might be "an unwarranted trespass on their sacred intellectual individuality." Dewey characterized such a method as "stupid" because it attempted the impossible and "misconceived the conditions of individual thinking." [12] Self-expression was cultivated before the pupils had anything to express and was confused with initiative and originality as truly creative. A sense of social responsibility and social understanding were expected to be acquired by osmosis, by participation in coöperative activities. The teacher was relegated to the position of a guide, counselor, or adviser on the assumption that any other position might smack of authoritarianism and dictation. Authoritarianism was confused with authority and order. As Dewey pointed out in an address at the Harvard Tercentenary Conference on Arts and Sciences, there was a failure to recognize that order and authority are essential to insure stability, on the one hand, and, on the other, freedom is necessary to make change possible. There is, said Dewey, "an intimate and organic union of the two things: of authority and freedom, of stability and change." [13]

The child-centered schools were, however, conventional, in the sense that they all seemed to engage in the same "creative" activities and forms of self-expression at the same time. In other respects they varied in character and emphasis from an exaggerated and excessive cult of freedom for the pupils, which Dewey often deplored, to schools that were genuinely experimental and pioneered in the development of certain aspects of the curriculum such as literature, art, and music. But in the latter case the work was done by exceptionally competent teachers who had a thorough mastery of the subjects that they taught and a sympathetic insight into the desirable needs of children.

The major characteristics of the progressive schools were formulated soon after its organization by the Progressive Education Association in 1919. They were as follows: attention to the child's physical well-being; opportunity for full development (initiative and self-expression in an environment rich in interesting material); social development and discipline (group consciousness developed through participation in the school as a community and discipline through self-mastery); beauty of environment; interest the motive of work; the curriculum (based on the nature and needs of childhood and youth, and acquisition of knowledge through scientific method of firsthand observation, investigation, experiment and research); the teacher as guide; scientific study of pupil development; coöperation between school and home; and the school as a contributor to educational progress.

The progressive movement undoubtedly had an important influence on the public schools, but a change had already been brought about by the American interpretation of Herbartianism and by the contributions of the newly developing psychology of education. The Herbartians, if they did not introduce radical changes in the curriculum, did stand for better teaching methods than were employed in the traditional schools. Through child study and educational psychology the followers of Herbart disseminated a better understanding of the growth of children and youth, of their interests and of the learning process, and of the importance of considering individual differences of ability.

The movement known as progressive education, inspired by the pragmatic philosophy, encouraged greater flexibility in the curriculum and coincided with the movement, stimulated by the new psychology, to include in the curricula and courses of study content that was immediately useful and meaningful to the pupil — in other words to teach such material as would be functional and had an instrumental value. There resulted from both movements a widespread tendency to revise the curriculum and to remake it, a tendency which prompted the emergence of curriculum experts to bring the content into line with the immediate interests of the pupils. Here as in so many other aspects of the educational revolution — emphasis on the needs and interests of the pupils and on the idea of freedom, for example — Dewey's doctrine was misinterpreted. On functionalism Dewey wrote in *Democracy and Education*, "Some goods are not good *for* anything; they are just goods. Any other notion leads to an absurdity. . . The proof of a good is found in the fact that the pupil responds; his response *is* use." [14]

Dewey's philosophy of education was interpreted and popularized by a number of disciples. Of these Dr. William H. Kilpatrick, professor of education, Teachers College, Columbia University, was undoubtedly the most influential in disseminating certain implications of Dewey's philosophy. He propagated the project method which was a crystallization of McMurry's *How To Study* and Dewey's *How We Think*, but placed the interests, problems, and purposes of the child at the center. The project method took the place, as a substitute, of general method, which in the Herbartian form of Five Formal Steps began to be discarded in favor of special methods. A project was defined as "any unit of purposeful activity where dominating purpose, as an inner urge, (1) fixes the aim (or end) of the action, (2) guides the process, (3) furnishes its drive, its inner motivation for its vigorous prosecution." When the plan of the project method was put forward in 1918, Kilpatrick was still an adherent of Thorndike's S.-R. bond theory and his laws of learning (readiness, exercise, and effect), which he was later to discard in favor of "organismic" psychology. The project method, however, was for several years more widely discussed than practiced.

THE NEW TRENDS UNDER CRITICISM

The vogue of the project method and of the child-centered school which emerged in the next decade did not pass unchallenged by educators who continued to recognize the importance of the cultural heritage of man and its value as an educational possession to be transmitted to oncoming generations. They saw also the value and significance of the new methods of education. They deplored, however, the chaotic character of an educational curriculum based on the child's interests and purposes, believing that the failure to select the content to be taught to pupils left a curriculum without values. The project method, they felt, was useful for certain subjects and on certain occasions but they believed that the teacher, professionally prepared, would employ any one of a number of methods, choosing the one most appropriate for a particular purpose. The activity method and curriculum and the project method left too much to chance and what was acquired in the way of knowledge incidental to the achievement of a purpose or the solution of a problem would not in their opinion be as easily retained in mind as when mastered through intelligent rather than mechanical drill and exercise. One of the leading educators who stood out in opposition to the radical trends was Professor William C. Bagley, a colleague of Professor Kilpatrick at Teachers College, Columbia University.

In 1935 a small group of educators, with Professor Bagley as their spokesman, formed themselves into a group called the Essentialist Committee whose central thesis was that to prepare the younger generation for their adult responsibilities systematic instruction in the fundamentals, in history, in English and other subjects was essential together with discipline and obedience when necessary. This thesis expressed definite opposition to the theory that stressed incidental learning through activities and experience as more appropriate to the development of independence, initiative, a sense of responsibility and self-discipline than formal and systematic curricular organization, discipline, and obedience. The essentialists were as interested in the progress and improvement of education as the progressives, but they preferred to lay the stress on raising the standards of the teaching profession and their preparation academically and professionally. They would have preferred to stand for education "with no qualifying adjectives prefixed," which Dewey regarded as the basic question.[15]

THE TEST OF THE DEPRESSION AND WAR YEARS

During the depression years in the thirties, elementary education like other branches of the educational system was seriously affected. For lack of funds school authorities in many areas were unable to pay the salaries of teachers and in some instances even to keep the schools open. Large numbers of children were for the time being deprived of schooling.

The full effects of these retrogressive conditions were not realized until the Selective Service was put into effect during World War II. The Service reported that 676,000 men of draft age were rejected for mental or educational deficiencies. This meant that they could not meet the standard of functional literacy which should have been attained after four years of education. Of the registrants for the draft 350,000 signed their names with a mark. Large numbers were drafted into the army with so little education that training in literacy skills had to be provided; the majority of those requiring such training were English-speaking. These deficiencies noted by the Selective Service were as much a handicap to war production as to military efficiency. In addition to those rejected for mental or educational deficiencies, about 30 per cent of the registrants were rejected for physical deficiencies which a sound system of health care at the school age might have noted and had corrected. Although not attributable to the lack of schooling in the depression period, the depressing picture of the educational status of the population revealed by the census of 1940 indicated that educational opportunities were either not provided or ignored. Of 73,725,819 persons over twenty-five years of age 2,799,923 or 3.8 per cent had not completed even one year of schooling, while 7,300,689 or 9.9 per cent had completed from one to four years. Thus a total of 10,104,612 or 13 per cent of those twenty-five years of age or over had less than five years of schooling. Nor was this poor showing due to the inadequate provision of schools in the southern states; the region with the best systems, the Pacific states, showed that 7.5 per cent of the population over twenty-five years of age had only one to four years of schooling.[16]

The period, however, was one of stocktaking and criticism. From the lay point of view, interested in reducing the cost of education, the schools were criticized for spending time and money on "fads and frills" and for attempting to take over the educational functions of agencies like the family and other social institutions. There was little justification for this kind of attack since what were called fads and frills had been introduced into the school program at the request of the public. This had been shown in 1911 by Dr. Walter A. Jessup in a study of *Social Factors Affecting Special Supervision*. Nevertheless, such subjects as art, physical education, home economics, and manual training were discarded from the curriculum of many elementary schools. Other charges against the schools were that the standards of discipline were low and that the curriculum was constantly being changed. On the other hand a committee, appointed in 1934 by the Board of Regents of the State of New York to inquire into elementary and secondary education, reported in 1938 that the schools of the state tended to ignore the cultural changes that were going on and that routine practices prevailed in the schools. The committee also expressed the opinion that the schools failed to provide the pupils with an adequate preparation for helpful participation in the state as citizens and in community, economic, and family life.[17]

Criticism of the type represented by the report of the New York State School Inquiry began to be generally heard as a protest against what was regarded as an overemphasis on individualism in the theory of the child-centered school and of progressive education, which had some influence in the public schools.

By the middle of the 'thirties the task of the Essentialist Committee, important as it was, and of other critics was already almost superfluous. Progressive education as formulated by the Progressive Education Association and as practiced in the child-centered schools was beginning to be subjected to critical examination by its friends who major attack was directed to its lack of a definite social aim and purpose. There were those who felt that progressive education in general had done little to prepare a generation for the problems of the depression years either in understanding the economic causes or with any idea of the types of changes that American society needed "to form an equitable and stable society," or for a civilization that "can give first place to finer and better things."

In 1932 Dr. George S. Counts, professor of education, Teachers College, Columbia University, published a challenge to the teaching profession and particularly to the progressive elements in it in a pamphlet with the significant title *Dare the School Build a New Social Order?* He was soon joined by many who had been recognized leaders in the progressive education movement and were themselves open to the criticisms leveled by Dr. Counts against progressive education. He charged that it had failed to elaborate a theory of social welfare "unless it be that of anarchy or extreme individualism" and had insisted that the school should be impartial and neutral. "Education," according to Dr. John L. Childs, a colleague of Dr. Counts, "will fail to make an important contribution to the reconstruction of our culture if it seeks to move no more rapidly than the approval of the whole community will permit." [18]

Two years before this statement was made, the leaders of the philosophy of progressive education had published *The Educational Frontier* as a profession of faith of the group. For the first time in the literature of progressive education the importance of values as well as of experimentation and change and a social point of view was stressed. The following statement is expressive of the change in attitude: "We have conceived that the office of a philosophy of education at the present time is to indicate the pressing need and to sketch the lines on which alone, in our conception, it can be met. The method of experimental intelligence as the method of action cannot be established as a constant and operative habit of mind and character apart from education. But it cannot be established within education except as the activities of the latter are founded on a clear idea of the active social forces of the day, of what they are doing, of their effect, for good and harm, upon others, and except as this idea and ideal are acted upon to direct experimentation in the currents of social life that run outside the school and that condition the effect and determine the educational meaning of whatever the school does." [19]

The educational situation during the depression years was too uncertain and unstable to introduce propaganda for a new social order even if there had been any agreement on the kind of order that was considered desirable. In a 1936 monograph on *Education and the Social Order* Dewey wrote: "There is an important difference between education *with respect to a new social order* and indoctrination into settled convictions about that order." [20] In 1934 the Commission on the Social Studies of the American Historical Association published its *Conclusions and Recommendations* after four years of investigation, although approval of the volume was not unanimous. The Commission, of which Dr. Counts was a member, concluded that "the age of individualism and *laissez faire* in economy and government is closing and that a new age of collectivism is emerging." Accordingly, the Commission believed that this view must furnish the educational background to prepare children and adults "for their coming trials, opportunities and responsibilities" without "neglecting precious elements in the traditional heritage of America and the world." The chief results of these and similar recommendations was to create unrest among teachers, increase the watchfulness of patriotic organizations suspicious of "strange tenets of government in the classrooms" and "ideas in the schoolroom of what is called a new social order."

It is impossible to determine with any degree of accuracy the extent to which the progressive philosophy of education was adopted in the schools of the country. The fact that the theory was widely disseminated and discussed does not provide sufficient evidence of its incorporation in classroom practice. One leader of the movement deplored, on the one hand, the conservatism of parents and school officials who stood in the way of remaking the schools "to a more adequate point of view," and on the other the persistence of "the miseducative trammels of subject-matter requirements, textbooks, promotions, grades, etc.," all of which stood in the way of a real experiment in education itself.[21] Dewey, however, recognized the first half of this century as a time of constant change in which relations between teachers and pupils had been humanized, discipline of the older kind had been abandoned, greater provision had been made for activity, indoctrination in the school subjects had become more skillful, and new subjects had been introduced. "Nevertheless," he went on to say, "there has been no fundamental change in spirit and motivation, either within the school or outside in society."[22]

If an explanation were needed of the apparent refusal to depart too radically from routine methods and from what society, which established them, expected from the schools, it will be found in the first paragraph of the Foreword of *The Purposes of Education in American Democracy*, issued by the Educational Policies Commission in 1938: "A million teachers in America have listened to addresses and read books, articles, reports, and courses of study on the purposes of education. These talks and publications fail to affect what is done in the classroom. One reason for their limited influence has been the tendency to deal in extremely broad generalizations which, for classroom procedures, could mean almost anything, and, therefore, mean almost nothing." [23]

The Commission continued a tradition that goes back to Herbert Spencer's classification of educational objectives on the basis of human activities, a practice followed by the Commission on the Reorganization of Secondary Education in its statement of the *Cardinal Principles of Secondary Education* (1918). The Commission identified four groups of objectives and proceeded to analyze the requirements to be met under each. The main objectives are set forth herewith, the implications being omitted:

The Objectives of Self-Realization: The inquiring mind; speech; reading, writing, number, sight and hearing; health knowledge and health habits, public health, recreation, intellectual interests, esthetic interests, character.

The Objectives of Human Relationship: Respect for humanity, friendship, coöperation, courtesy, appreciation of the home, conservation of the home, homemaking, democracy in the home.

The Objectives of Economic Efficiency: Work, occupational information, occupational choice, occupational efficiency, occupational appreciation, personal economics, consumer judgment, efficiency in buying, consumer protection.

The Objectives of Civic Responsibility: Social justice, social activity, social understanding, critical judgment, tolerance, conservation, social application of science, world citizenship, law observance, economic literacy, political citizenship, devotion to democracy.[24]

These objectives come near to a definition of the objectives of education as actually incorporated in the curricula and courses of study of the majority of the nation's school systems and in the textbooks that are used than all the literature on the cultivation of attitudes, dispositions, originality, and creativity.

THE COMMUNITY-CENTERED SCHOOL

The objectives defined by the commission fitted in with the new emphasis inspired, on the one hand, by criticisms of the child-centered school, and on the other by the spread of the movement to teach the social studies and to train for active and intelligent participation in the tasks and duties of citizenship. The new trend was to the community-centered school, which seeks to find the content of education in the manifold activities and experiences of the local community, the topics being selected, according to the ages of the pupils, from an expanding community — local, national, and international. Trips and excursions to museums, farms, factories, and local agencies of government are expected to provide experiences that could not be derived from books and make the school studies more real and concrete. The community-centered school began to be advocated in 1932.

In 1938 the Society for Curriculum Study issued a volume on *The Community School* the main theses of which were as follows: All life is education, which is not limited to the schools. Schools should be concerned with the improvement of the community and of the social order. The major problems of the community should provide the orientation for education. The common concerns of individuals and social groups would make for progress in education and community living. An education based on community problems is more important than the perpetuation of academic traditions and practices. Democratic processes and ideals should be the basis of relations between teachers and pupils.[25]

The community-centered theory became the dominant note in education for the next two decades, except for the years when the threat of war and World War II broadened the scope of the theory to a consideration of national and world affairs and particularly to the problems involved in the preservation of democracy. In August, 1939, a Congress on Education for Democracy was held at Teachers College, Columbia University, and was attended by representatives from the leading American national organizations and from the democratic nations of Europe. The discussion reinforced the thesis that democracy cannot be taken for granted and must determine every aspect of education. Democracy had already served as the theme of a number of publications of the Educational Policies Commission of the National Education Association and the American Association of School Administrators. The commission on the outbreak of World War II directed attention to issues of Education for National Defense.[26]

Education as an essential basis for national defense and the preservation of democracy reinforced the theory of the community-centered school. The theory stressed the idea that the school has a social role and must, therefore, cultivate close relations with its community and become an integral part of its activities and interests. The activities of the school must be based on the actual needs and problems of a community rather than on the transitory and so-called spontaneous needs and interests of the children. Since problems can only be solved by the process of education, the school can become an agency for the betterment of a community and provide through the teachers and pupils the initiative for the conduct of activities and enterprises for community improvement. Examples that have been cited as proper for study in the elementary school have included the high costs of living and housing problems with trips to slums and public housing projects. In this way, it is claimed, pupils have realistic and significant experiences at first hand and not through books or audio-visual materials. In fact the community-centered school shares one point in common with the child-centered school in that both are protests against book-learning in favor of real life activities. The only difference between them is in the source of the activities; in one case the source comes from the felt needs of the child, and in the other from the real needs of the community which the child is assumed to share with adults. The school becomes a center of social action and "a service institution devoted to improve the quality of life lived by all the people of the community." [27]

The community becomes a laboratory for the school and teachers must become familiar with the resources and facilities that are available which may include the following: "Points of historical interest, industries and businesses which can be studied, governmental agencies, civic institutions, geographical characteristics, natural resources, flora and fauna, conditions affecting health, social problems of housing, of zoning, of streets, of water supply and of conservation, and transportation and traffic conditions are all examples of community factors which are grist to the mill of a life-centered learning program." [28] Where pupils are to get an idea of the standards and values for improving life in their community is nowhere discussed.

There appear to be two basic premises which the educational theory of the past two decades has attempted to reconcile. On the one hand it emphasizes that the individual is unique and must be allowed to develop and cultivate originality, creativity, initiative, and inventivness in order to be ready to meet the problems of a rapidly changing situation. The qualities mentioned, it is claimed, represent the central ideal of democracy.[29] To disregard this ideal is to deprive the individual of the opportunity to exercise his freedom. By contrast, it was charged that the traditional practices of education cultivated habits, routine, conformity, and conventionality by means of rigid discipline, rote learning, memorization, and indoctrination. How the progress of American culture has been achieved under such a standardized and authoritarian type of education is never explained. It is enough for the advocates of the new, the progressive, and the modern to rest their case on a rejection of the tradition as they conceive it to have been carried on.

The second of the two premises is that the content of schoolwork must not be sought in the immediate and transitory needs of children but in the resources of the community and its problems in the solution of which teachers, pupils, and citizens should participate. It is significant that it is only the rare treatise on the theory of elementary education that mentions subjects that a pupil ought to be taught or, since teaching has in theory become mainly guidance, subjects that a pupil should learn. For the important ends of education do not consist in the acquisition of "mere" knowledge, facts, and information, but in the development of conduct and behavior in democratic human relations, coöperation in group activities, initiative, research methods, and critical-mindedness.[30]

The child-centered school was criticized for its overemphasis of individualism. The community-centered school may end by overemphasizing the adjustment of the individual to a society, which is already under criticism for putting a premium on conformity. How far this adjustment of the individual could be carried may be gathered from the following statements in a Yearbook issued in 1947 by the American Association of School Administrators on *Schools for A New World*: "The supreme problem is the retention among other things of a democratic order in which individual lives merge in a supreme entity of purpose and being that in itself is the ultimate goal. . . This means a shift in emphasis from helping the individual in his own right to become a valuable member of society to the preparation of the individual to the realization of his best self in the higher loyalty of serving the basic ideals and aims of society, the individual who can voluntarily put community before self." [31]

THEORY AND PRACTICE

The trends in educational theory may not give a clue to what is actually being done in the classrooms of the public elementary schools. The theorists frequently complain that teachers soon fall into routine habits and prefer the security of the customary to experimenting with innovations. On the other hand, theories are too frequently put forward by writers who have had little or no direct experience in teaching young children. A recent report, *Elementary School Objectives*, prepared by Nolan C. Kearney for the Mid-Century Committee on Elementary Education presented a list of questions that come closer to the practical situations than the educational theory of the last few decades: "(a) What should children know, remember, understand? (b) What skills should they perfect to the point of performance with little pause for thought? (3) What competences should they have in the way of solving problems, thinking clearly on the basis of reliable evidence? (d) What attitudes and interests are most valuable? (e) What values should children hold? (f) What general habit patterns and what methods of attack on problems should be developed? (g) What are the limitations set by nature and culture that the schools (and the children) cannot be expected to overcome?" [32] These are practical questions that school principals and teachers as well as parents would wish to ask.

A list of the common needs of children in the seventh and eighth grades which was presented in a U.S. Office of Education publication and was based on information supplied by the administration and their staffs in fifty-four public-school systems was another indication that the "new and modern" had not displaced some of the more essential elements that apparently have been discarded by the innovators in educational theory. The common needs were stated to be the following:

(1) Environmental conditions to maintain healthy, growing bodies. (2) Individualized program of activity and rest to nurture health and growth in every child. (3) Program of health services, practices, and instruction to secure for each individual optimum health, protection from disease and accident, and correction of defects, and to educate children in the care of their bodies. (4) Conditions to enable children to gain the affection and friend-ship of those upon whom they depend for the sense of security and worth, and to develop the attitudes and skills which are funda-mental to a sense of security. (5) Conditions to help each child develop a sense of worth and self-respect by meeting the demands of the environment in whatever things the society holds in high value. (6) A school program to meet the needs of each child, aiming ultimately at self-guidance and independence. (7) Cur-riculum opportunity to help each grow continuously in basic academic skills, understandings powers of expression, emotional resources, and working with others.[33]

Nor have the latest theories found their way into official courses of study. The course of study for the upper elemen-tary-school division of the State of Oregon, issued in 1953 by the State Board of Education, contained the following para-graph in a Foreword by the Superintendent of Public In-struction, Rex Putnam: "Within these pages will be found the philosophy upon which child development in Oregon is based, a suggested scope of material and experience, and a statement of some of the reasonable attainments to be ex-pected from the child at certain age levels. These and many other features of the guide help to implement the State Board of Education action of December 18, 1952, when the motion was passed, 'That in curriculum building and supervision the State Board of Education recommends a thorough mastery on the proper levels of such fundamental subjects as language arts, mathematics, history, geography, science, and hygiene.' " The Guide, which was "the result of the work, thoughtful consideration, and constructive criticisms of numerous class-room teachers and administrators throughout the State," describes the curriculum of Grades Seven and Eight by subjects (social studies, arts of communication, arithmetic, science, health education, physical education, art, and music).[34]

The "Foreword" to a bulletin, published in 1954 by the Bureau of Elementary Curriculum Development of the New York State Education Department and issued to help local communities to work out their own courses of study, stated that the bulletin "highlights by grades and by subjects recommendations and suggestions which the State Education Department is making to the elementary schools through handbooks, bulletins, pamphlets, supervisory letters, child development aids, and other publications now in use in the schools or projected for use in the immediate future. It describes a program that has been developing in New York State during the past ten years." After referring to individual differences among children it dealt with their common needs. "It outlines the common learnings — learnings such as the citizenship practices and understandings which are vital to Americans; the science knowledge essential to survival in the modern world; and such fundamentals as reading, writing, numbers, spelling, history, geography, health practices and our common heritage in the arts (music, fine and practical arts). The bulletin also discusses other needs of children which schools must satisfy. It outlines what society wants children to know. It describes what children are like and how they learn. It presents, in effect a design for the elementary curriculum." [35]

The New Primary Manual: A Teacher's Guide, prepared by a committee of teachers of the public schools of Cincinnati, Ohio, "presents a more distinct view of the basic purposes of primary education, more concrete help in the development of the fundamental skills, more emphasis on appreciation of America, and a more consistent picture which each instructional area makes to the program as a whole." The Manual, intended for teachers of the kindergarten and Grades One, Two and Three, described the curriculum even at this stage in terms of subjects — language arts, reading, arithmetic,

social studies, science, physical education, music, and art.[36]
What society wants children to know is based on the recollection by parents of what they themselves had been taught in their school days and by requirements imposed by state laws. Legislative requirements are more extensive than is normally understood. They include the three R's, citizenship and civil government, United States Constitution and history, geography, grammar, physiology and hygiene including anti-alcoholism, and physical training. Humane treatment of animals, state history, health, and music are other subjects that are required by law but not as generally as the other subjects listed.[37]

Even where subjects as such have been retained in the curriculum, variations have taken place in the organization of the course of study. When the time schedule has been arranged by subjects, the objection has been raised that the work of a day was too fragmented and that there was a failure to show how the subjects were related to each other. To correct this situation the plan of correlation was developed, as described earlier. A further step was to organize the subjects into "broad fields" or "cores," or fused or integrated, a practice which may have been inspired by the project method or by the fusion of history, geography, and civics into social studies. Undoubtedly the current developments can be traced back to such methods of organization as correlation, or by topics and types. The "unit" arrangement of lessons is an example of the same trend. There is retained in the varieties of organization a consciousness of the value and importance of fundamental subjects. By contrast the "area of living" or "life-situations" curriculum relegated subjects, knowledge, facts, and information to a subordinate place, and stressed outcomes of every kind except the intellectual. Activity methods are used but not exclusively. A sound system permits the teacher who is well-prepared to utilize any method of instruction that may seem appropriate for any

lesson. The notion that nothing of any value, whether intellectual or emotional, takes place in the pupil or that no influence is exercised on the pupil's behavior when "passive"
methods are used is gradually being surrendered. This idea
about passive methods has been as much a fiction as the concept about traditional education with which students of education have been indoctrinated by leaders who have themselves employed the subtlest methods of indoctrination.

The standards of attainment of elementary school pupils
have, as previously mentioned, been seriously questioned by
the public since World War II. The schools have always
been subjected to criticism, but never to the degree attained
in the recent decades. The situation in this period may be the
result of conditions that have affected the schools adversely
— the economic depression and the war years, the shortage
of classrooms and teachers, and the consequent oversized
classes or double sessions which more recently have been due
to the increased birth rate. Many of the critics have blamed
progressive education for the low standards of attainment,
and the depreciation by the "modern" theory of education
of "knowledge as an end" may bear some responsibility for
producing some uncertainty among teachers about the utiliza-
tion of new or old methods.

To the complaints of parents and employers that the products of the schools cannot read, write, or spell, and are uncertain in their arithmetic, the stock answer is that "research
shows" that modern children can do better than their predecessors of the same age and grade on old examination papers
that had been written in the earlier period. Nevertheless,
high-school teachers who have the responsibility of continuing the education of modern children complain that incom-
petence in the fundamentals makes it impossible for many of
them to derive any profit from their stay in school. It is frequently admitted, first, that the high school is trying to give
some form of secondary education to pupils who have only

fourth-, fifth-, or sixth-grade reading and arithmetic ability, and second that about 60 per cent of the pupils in high schools are wasting their time and making no progress in education. (See Chapter IV.) To this the usual rebuttal is: first, that high-school teachers are still wedded to the academic point of view; second, that high-school pedagogy has not yet caught up with modern theory; and, third, that the high schools today are attended by a vast number of pupils who a generation ago would never have entered them.

Whatever the reasons for the poor standards, the fact remains that educational authorities have had to recognize the deficiencies in the fundamental subjects by organizing remedial classes in reading and arithmetic at every level of the educational system, including remedial classes or clinics in reading in college. The concern about the successful teaching of reading can best be indicated by the fact that more than two thousand studies have been published embodying the results of research into methods of teaching the subject. The criticisms of the low attainments may be unpalatable, but cannot be brushed aside, when other incontrovertible facts in the educational system and in such an extensive test on a nation-wide scale as the Selective Service can be cited.

The results of the system might have been poorer than the critics allege if the tests had not been introduced to measure achievement in practically every activity of the elementary school. The tests may have been used for wrong purposes — for standardization or to measure the competence of teachers. When used as they were intended to be used — to discover or to diagnose pupils' difficulties or inadequacies of teaching methods, the employment of tests justified itself. A tendency has developed to depreciate the value of such measurement through the use of tests on the ground that the tests may determine the aim of education, particularly in terms of the acquisition of knowledge. This tendency has been accompanied by a movement to substitute evaluation for measure-

ment. Evaluation, it is argued, implies a definition of values
or a philosophy of education against which the appraisal of
the work and outcomes of a class or school can be appraised.
There is measurement in this method but it is qualitative, in
terms of growth and behavior and development on lines other
than intellectual, rather than quantitative in terms only of
intellectual attainments.

Connected with this movement in favor of qualitative
evaluation is the revolt against using marks as a measure of
pupil achievement. Marks, it is argued, are measures of a one-
sided curriculum objective — the intellectual — which is not
suited to modern education. Marks do not measure the progress of pupils in intangible outcomes that are desirable, such
as ability and growth in democratic living and social competence. They may show a pupil's standing in relation to other
pupils in a class and his readiness at the end of a period for
promotion or otherwise. But the standards are false standards
since the marks cannot indicate a pupil's strength or weakness
even in the different operations in arithmetic or the different
elements of a composition. They set up wrong kinds of motivation and are as likely to discourage some pupils as to encourage others. Further, they are socially unsound, since
they encourage competition among pupils and may develop
a superiority or inferiority complex, neither of which is desirable in a well-rounded personality. Finally, whatever system of marking may be used — percentages or literal marks
or qualitative statements — the results are objected to as un-
reliable.

The chief objection to the use of marks is that they are
adapted only to one educational aim — the acquisition of
knowledge, facts, and information, a one-sided aim. They do
not take account of other outcomes and objectives that include
the total development and growth of a pupil. A school report
should contain information not on where the pupil stands in
relation to others or to arbitrarily defined standards of achieve-

ment, but should be broken down into meaningful information on the many-sided possibilities of progress and growth
as well as of improvement. Accordingly, it is urged that more
extensive and detailed records be kept and that conferences
be arranged between teachers and parents, which serve the
end of linking school and home, eliciting information about
a pupil's home background, and helping parents understand
what the school is trying to do in terms of objectives and
outcomes. But as the authors wrote in a book recently published, "tradition has left an almost indelible imprint on the
thinking of members of the teaching profession, as well as
upon the thinking of laymen, with respect to the nature and
scope of pupil evaluation." [38] Parents appear to be sceptical
about the newer kinds of education and prefer old-fashioned
marks.

Another indirect result of the emphasis on the individual-
ization of education is the uncertainty about the classification
and grouping of pupils and consequently about the system
of grades into which the eight years of elementary education
have been divided. The problem is, indeed, not new. The
work of Francis W. Parker became known first for his practice of providing assistants to the teachers in each class in
Quincy, Massachusetts, to help backward pupils. A variety of
plans to break down the lockstep system of grouping pupils
by grades has been tried out in the past fifty years — the
Pueblo, Colorado, individual progress plan; the Batavia, New
York, plan of special assistance to slow pupils; the Cambridge,
Massachusetts, and Portland, Oregon, plan of allowing able
pupils to complete the eight-year course in six years; the
contrast or unit plans of Winnetka, Illinois, and Dalton,
Massachusetts, developed respectively by Carleton Washburn
and Helen Parkhurst; and the X.Y.Z. plan of ability grouping
of Detroit. The eight-grade system of classification and the
recognition of individual differences have also led to various
practices in promoting pupils annually or semi-annually. More

recently experiments have been conducted with three or four-
year flexible units, generally at the kindergarten-primary
level, with considerable freedom left to the teachers to adjust
the work to the abilities of the individual pupils and permitting
the arrangement of groups for coöperative work. According
to the latest theory, objection is raised against homogeneous
grouping of pupils according to ability because it is a vestige
of the traditional emphasis on the mastery of subjects. The
heterogeneous grouping of pupils is advocated as more representative of a democratic society which seeks to provide
freedom of development for each individual and is more in
accord with modern theories of education. In such a system
it is argued that groupings within a class or within several
classes would develop naturally according to common interests and needs.

The idea common to all recent theories is that elementary
education has its own ends in terms of children's needs and
abilities, that it should be devoted to a continuous process of
promoting the growth and development of each child's personality, physically, morally, emotionally, intellectually, and
socially. Preparation for work in the secondary schools
through mastery of the fundamentals should not dominate the
work of the elementary schools.

In the first chapter of this book the statement was made
that education today is characterized by confusion and uncertainty. The present chapter has traced the development of
a number of conflicting theories of elementary education
which have produced this confusion in the minds not only of
parents and the public, but also of members of the profession.
That many teachers have not wished to pursue every new
trend can be gathered from the frequent references by the
innovaters or "man-milliners in education" to the teachers'
fear of new ideas and their preference for routine practices
to which they have become accustomed. In the last few years,
the criticisms from lay groups have mounted in number. But

too often the professional leaders instead of examining the criticisms dispassionately resent them and are complacent about the results. Criticisms are brushed aside as emanating from the "enemies" of public education, and no attempt is made to disentangle those that are unwarranted and motivated by ill-concealed prejudices from those that are legitimate and based on principles of education, culture, and democracy whose stability cannot be shaken.

So far as current trends are concerned the development of theories of elementary education appear to have followed the pattern of other aspects of modern culture. The proponents are looking for an education without form or tone or standards except those that would make the individual the measure of all things, and the goal may have been reached in the introduction in one school system of the "Pupil Self-Appraisal Form."

CHAPTER IV

Education of the Adolescent

EQUALITY OF EDUCATIONAL OPPORTUNITIES: ITS CONSEQUENCES

The most striking expression of the faith of the American people in education is the provision of equality of educational opportunity for boys and girls between the ages of fourteen and seventeen. While the aim of providing such opportunity for all adolescents has not yet been reached, the United States, with seventy-five per cent of its adolescents enrolled in the high schools, has far outstripped other countries in the provision of postprimary education. The provision of equality of educational opportunities for all Americans is, indeed, regarded as one of the essential characteristics of democracy. The achievement of the ideal has, however, brought in its train a series of problems for which educators have sought to find solutions for at least half a century. For while it has not been difficult to secure the provision of more and more high-school buildings, the type of instruction to be given to the increasing number of youth in the schools with individual differences of intellectual capacity and different occupational destinations as well as with different social, economic, and cultural backgrounds has not been simple to determine. The American faith in education has become translated into the slogan "Give every boy and girl a chance." Beyond that, however, confusion and uncertainty have prevailed regarding the curricula and courses to be offered.

The term "secondary education," which is still used to

refer to the education given to pupils in high schools, has lost all resemblance to its traditional connotation. Traditionally, it implied a curriculum consisting of the mother tongue, one or more foreign languages (ancient or modern), history and geography, mathematics and science, and physical education. Such a curriculum was intended for a minority who had the ability to profit by it. It was the academic or college preparatory curriculum and was characteristic of secondary education throughout the nineteenth century, and still constitutes the major requirement for entrance to college. When the Committee of Ten, appointed by the National Education Association, issued its report in 1893, this curriculum was understood to be suitable for all students irrespective of their destination, whether college or some other career, partly since it was a good medium for mental discipline and partly since it was an introduction to liberal education.

The Committee of Ten could not foresee, however, that within a few decades the high schools would begin to be attended by pupils who neither by intellectual ability nor by interest or inclination could profit by pursuing the academic course. The unrest in secondary education began in the early years of this century when it was found that pupils dropped out of high schools without completing the course or failed to meet the requirements for graduation if they continued to the end of the four-year course.

During the same period in the first decade of this century, one of the claims on which the value of the traditional curriculum was based was that if the pupil did not profit by studying it, at least the discipline itself helped to train the mind and the mind so trained could successfully be applied to other activities, whether intellectual or practical. The psychologists of the day proved that the exaggerated claims made for such formal discipline and transfer of training were not valid. The results of the investigations were vague enough to lead to the interpretation that the doctrine of formal discipline and transfer of training had been "exploded" forever, although the psychologists themselves put forward no such rash claim. But the idea of an "explosion" came opportunely at a time when, because of increasing enrollments, high schools were ready to expand their programs of studies and administrators could speed up the development of more high schools by promising the public that new courses and new subjects could now be added to meet the needs and interests of the pupils and thus encourage them to remain longer in school. For this promise the administrators found support in the recommendation of the Committee of Ten that "all the subjects between which choice is allowed should be approximately equivalent to each other in seriousness, dignity, and efficiency." The quantitative measure of subjects or the recognition of the equivalence of all subjects taught for the same length of time was intended by this Committee and by the Committee on College Entrance Requirements (1899) to apply only to a limited number of subjects. But the door was thus opened for the introduction of a host of other subjects which, if taught for the same length of time, were considered to be equal in value to the traditional subjects. In the end, all sense of the educational value of subjects excepting insofar as it meets the needs of pupils disappeared.

Two other principles, enunciated by the Committee on College Entrance Requirements, came to the support of those who saw an opportunity to expand the "offerings" of the high schools. These principles were, first, that "throughout the course of secondary instruction surely there must be no Procrustean bed which every pupil by some process of dwarfing or stretching must be made to fit, but natural endowments, as soon as discovered, should have full scope, within certain limitations." The second principle was that "the secondary schools are the schools of the people, and the people have demanded and in still more effectual ways will demand, that their courses be practical, beneficial, disciplinary."

The reports of these Committees, the assumed explosion or total demolition of the doctrine of formal discipline and transfer of training, the approval of the elective system and the statistical study of elimination of students during the course and mortality or failure to graduate combined with the changes that were beginning to be noticed in American culture helped to hasten the day when the traditional faith in education could be translated into a more extensive provision of equality of educational opportunities for all. Among the changes that were taking place were the rapidity of industrialization and mechanization of industrial processes and the development of mass production which added momentum to the urbanization of the population. The old frontier had been conquered before the end of the nineteenth century; a new frontier was now being developed and was constantly being pushed forward. The significant changes that took place between 1890 and 1952 in secondary education are shown in Table A.

The increased wealth of the country made it possible to secure more funds for education and consequently for the provision of more high schools. The increase in income enabled families to dispense with wages earned by their children and to keep them longer in school, while the growing mechanization of industry and the influence of labor unions made it difficult for young persons to secure employment of a satisfactory character. The opportunity was seized in many states to raise the age of compulsory school attendance until today pupils must remain in school until ages ranging from fifteen to eighteen with dispensation of a year in some localities if satisfactory employment has been obtained.

THE COMPREHENSIVE HIGH SCHOOL

There were certain conditions under which secondary education as generally understood gradually began to change its character and became in a broad sense the education of

Table A.—Historical statistics of public secondary day schools: 1890–1952

[Junior high schools are included, beginning in 1920. Ungraded schools and schools with fewer than 10 pupils are included, beginning in 1938]

Item	1890	1900	1910	1920	1930	1938	1946	1952
1	2	3	4	5	6	7	8	9
Number of schools on file___					23,930	25,308	24,146	23,757
Schools reporting_____	2,526	6,005	10,213	14,326	22,237	25,091	24,146	23,757
Pupils in grades 7–12_____	202,963	519,251	915,061	1,999,106	5,212,179	7,458,045	6,861,030	7,693,140
Boys_____	85,943	216,207	398,525	891,469	2,522,816	3,633,319	3,248,960	3,797,550
Girls_____	117,020	303,044	516,536	1,107,637	2,689,363	3,824,726	3,612,070	3,895,590
Percent girls_____	57.7	58.4	56.4	55.4	51.6	51.3	52.6	50.6
Teachers_____	9,120	20,372	41,667	97,654	213,306	274,163	1 286,512	332,106
Men_____	3,695	10,172	18,890	34,396	74,532	113,249	104,886	151,575
Women_____	5,425	10,200	22,777	63,258	138,774	160,914	181,626	180,531
Percent women_____	59.5	50.1	54.7	64.8	65.1	58.7	63.4	54.4
Average number of teachers per school_____	3.6	3.4	4.1	6.8	9.6	10.9	11.9	14.0
Average number of pupils per school_____	80.3	86.5	89.6	139.5	234.4	297.2	284.1	323.8
Average number of pupils per teacher_____	22.3	25.5	22.0	20.5	24.4	27.2	23.9	23.2
Pupils in last 4 years of high school [2]_____	202,963	519,251	915,061	1,851,965	4,135,171	5,926,722	5,417,122	5,695,514
Boys_____	85,943	216,207	398,525	821,015	1,986,246	2,852,539	2,615,658	2,785,553
Girls_____	117,020	303,044	516,536	1,030,950	2,148,925	3,074,183	2,801,464	2,909,961
Percent girls_____	57.7	58.4	56.4	55.7	52.0	51.9	51.7	51.1
Population, aged 14–17 years [3]_____	5,354,653	6,152,231	7,220,298	7,735,841	9,341,221	9,908,000	8,897,000	8,728,000
Percent of population, aged 14–17 years in last 4 years of high school_____	3.8	8.4	12.7	23.9	44.3	59.8	60.9	65.3
High-school graduates_____	21,882	61,737	111,363	230,902	591,719	1,030,216	1,011,173	4 1,045,633
Boys_____	7,692	22,575	43,657	90,516	267,298	481,457	442,214	496,087
Girls_____	14,190	39,162	67,706	140,386	324,421	548,759	568,959	549,546
Percent girls_____	64.8	63.4	60.8	60.8	54.8	53.3	56.3	52.6

1 Includes not only teachers but also, in the case of the 24 ungraded schools, other professional staff (principals, supervisors, counselors, etc.).
2 Includes special or unclassified pupils of high-school grade.
3 Bureau of the Census. Data for the years 1938–52 estimated by the Bureau.
4 Data are for the school year 1950–51. Sex distribution estimated.

NOTE.—The figures in italics represent revisions of previously published data. The data have been revised to exclude postgraduates from "Pupils in the last 4 years of high school," 1920–46; to include schools enrolling fewer than 10 pupils, 1938 and 1946; and to exclude evening schools, 1938 and 1946. The data for 1930 and presumably for prior years include some evening schools.

[This Table is reproduced from Statistics of Public Secondary Day Schools, 1951–52, U. S. Department of Health, Education, and Welfare, Office of Education (Washington, D.C., 1954), p. 6.]

the adolescent, or, in the terminology more recently adopted, the education of *all* American youth. At first the program of studies recognized by tradition and by the two committees mentioned earlier as the curriculum of secondary education was continued. Then new types of courses of a more practical or technical character were established here and there – in separate schools and afterwards side by side with the academic course. Distances and other causes led the public to demand that high schools should provide all types of courses in the same buildings to suit the needs and to be closer to the homes of a growing clientele. The comprehensive or cosmopolitan high school thus originated in public demand; the rationalization came subsequently that such a school for all adolescents, irrespective of differences of ability or destination, is more democratic and makes for social solidarity. It is perhaps not an exaggeration to see here not only the fact that the payer called the tune, but also that a public accustomed to find everything it wants in one store should expect to do the same in the school. The comprehensive high school also represented a movement to break down the monopoly of the traditional academic course. Administrators readily accommodated the schools to the wishes of the public and to newly emerging social demands and introduced such a variety of subjects that 274 courses were reported about 1950 by the United States Office of Education as available in the high schools of the country. Since for graduation from high school with a general certificate all subjects taught for the same length of time were equal, the number need not be surprising.

The curriculum was expanded to include agriculture, home economics, and vocational studies; attention began to be given to such subjects as health, music, and art and their appreciation, and older subjects were integrated into general mathematics, general science, and social studies (history, geography, civics, and economics) intended partly to break down the fractioning of the curriculum into compartments and partly to provide a general orientation into various areas of learning. In 1917, a stimulus was given to the development of practical arts and vocational subjects by the Smith-Hughes Act which provided the grant of federal funds for the encouragement of instruction in trades, agriculture, and home economics.

At the end of the first decade of the century, the junior high school was already in the process of being established in the larger urban areas. A division of the traditional twelve years of the common school into two six-year periods instead of the eight- and four-year periods had been advocated by President Charles W. Eliot in 1888 and by the Committee of Ten of the National Education Association and the Committee on College Entrance Requirements. Originally recommended in order to provide a longer period of secondary education, the junior high school, when established, was intended to make the transition from the grades to high school easier and to provide a period of exploration on the basis of which pupils could specialize in the senior high school. The first of these two aims has been continued but for the rest the work of the junior and senior high school, whether they are separate in two three-year periods or in one six-year period, is now considered from a unitary point of view. In discussions of high-school problems it is difficult to discover whether the four or six-year high school is under consideration. The majority of pupils still attend the four-year high school, but the transition from the grades is facilitated in the last two years, the intermediate grades, of the elementary schools, now supervised by the U.S. Office of Education.

The consequence of all the trends and influences discussed was that, except for college entrance requirements, graduation from high school came to mean that a certain number of points had been accumulated in a number of discrete subjects and that there was lacking a philosophy of education at this stage. Education of the individual for personal development was substituted for the aim of imparting culture or a liberal education, since it was alleged that these terms had become too ambiguous and indefinite.

REORGANIZATION OF SECONDARY EDUCATION

In an effort to check the drift the National Education Association in 1913 appointed a Commission on the Reorganization of Secondary Education. One of the purposes of the Commission was to "formulate statements of valid aims, efficient methods, and kinds of materials whereby each subject may best serve the needs of high school pupils." The general report of the commission, *Cardinal Principles of Education*, appeared in 1918 and ushered in a new trend in the consideration of the problems of adolescent education, a trend which had already been forecast in the period of unrest beginning in the opening years of the century and which is still under way under the name of "education for life adjustment," which is a latter-day embellishment of the "cardinal principles."

Attention was drawn at that time, as it has been drawn in every publication on the subject since then, to the growing complexity of community life, to the relation of the individual to state, national, and international affairs, to the development of specialization in industry, to the changing character of family and home life, and to the importance of training for the use of leisure time. The problems of secondary education were summarized in the following statements: "(1) The purpose of democracy is so to organize society that each member may develop his personality primarily through activities designed for the well-being of his fellow-members and of society as a whole. (2) Education in a democracy, both within and without the school, should develop in each individual the knowledge, interests, ideals, habits, and powers, whereby he will find his place and use that place to shape both himself and society toward ever nobler ends." The "nobler ends" were nowhere defined!

The definition of the objectives of secondary education, however, became the slogan for all workers in that field, and it has persisted to the present, while much that was written by the subject-matter committees appointed by the commission and a few years later by other special committees were ignored. These reports included *Report on the Reorganization of Mathematics in Secondary Education* (1923) by the National Committee on Mathematical Requirements of the Mathematical Association, the *Classical Investigation* (1925) by the Advisory Committee of the American Classical League; and *Reports on Modern Language Teaching* (1929 and 1930) by the American and Canadian Committees on Modern Languages. History and social studies were dealt with in the report of the Commission on Social Studies of the American Historical Association. All the specialist reports were outstanding and aroused a great deal of interest, but they were published at a time when the objectives of secondary education were being reorganized. Hence their influence was not as great as that of the specialist reports published at the end of the nineteenth century. In the first place the number of offerings in the high schools had increased considerably. And second, candidates for appointment were in a majority of cases certificated as high-school teachers and had to teach any subject assigned to them; they were not specialists except in the larger school systems.

The objectives which the curricula of high schools were to be organized to promote were as follows: (1) health; (2) command of fundamental processes; (3) worthy home-membership; (4) vocation; (5) civic education; (6) worthy use of leisure; and (7) ethical character. The objectives were intended to promote a unitary and continuous process in education and to help in the interrelation of subjects. They had no noticeable effect, however, on the courses of secondary education in practice. But attention was shifted from subjects to be taught to a consideration of "outcomes" of

education in terms of meeting life needs. The statement on
cardinal principles reflected the new trend in educational
philosophy which emphasized growth, the experiences of the
pupils as the starting point in their education, and their active
participation because they understood what they were learning. The statement on the cardinal principles also fitted in
with a movement initiated by still another Committee of the
National Education Association — the Committee on Economy of Time appointed in 1911. In four reports, issued from
1915 to 1919, the committee, utilizing the new "scientific"
methods of analyzing the needs of an individual in adult life,
sought, as Herbert Spencer had sought earlier, to discover
"What Knowledge Is of Most Worth?" That quest, as will
appear in the account that follows, has been continued to the
present and educational history since then been filled with
the statement of thousands of "objectives" until their culmination in the statement by the Educational Policies Commission in 1944 of "ten imperative needs of youth."

The emphasis of the commission on life needs and outcomes rather than on subjects and the importance attached
to the task of encouraging boys and girls to remain in school
to the age of eighteen was to be developed in greater detail
in the years that followed. The new point of view gave support to those who were ready to attack the traditional curriculum of the secondary school as static and conservative,
as designed for the privileged minority and therefore "aristocratic," as futile and useless or "decorative" and meaningless
in the light of the great cultural changes that have taken place
in the present century. Along the same lines were the criticism that the academic course dealt with abstract learning
and symbols and was "bookish" and verbal. The gravamen
of the attacks was the college-entrance requirements and the
notion implicit in the report of the Committee of Ten that
the subjects required for college entrance were good for all
pupils irrespective of their destination.

In attacking the traditional academic curriculum, however, the proponents of a different type of education for all adolescents to prepare them for life in a changing cultural age were repeating the history of the attacks on education following the American Revolution between 1776 and 1800. They disregarded the remarkable progress of this country in the nineteenth century despite the fact that the changes advocated by the radicals in the infant years of the Republic had little effect. To get a proper perspective on the current issue it is important to bear in mind the traditional influences in American education and the cultural background responsible for them. It will be found that, despite all the parading of the new theories to give point to the argument for an education to meet the new needs of adolescents in a new environment, the charges against the academic curriculum are in fact not new.

THE TRADITION OF ANTI-INTELLECTUALISM

The educational crisis which is the subject of widespread concern and discussion today is not the result of newfangled theories of education; it has its roots in the history of American civilization and culture. The crisis has not been sprung upon the educational world suddenly; it is the product of conflicts in American education which can be traced back to the middle of the eighteenth century. Nor has it arisen because of new demands of American society resulting from the development of the sciences, technology, and new economic and social needs in recent decades. The unrest has been persistent in American cultural history; it was marked in the early years of the Republic by the conflict between Jeffersonianism and Jacksonianism, between the cult of the "aristoi" and the needs of the common man. This unrest, usually ascribed to changing cultural conditions and the individual differences in ability and needs of the increased number of pupils in high schools, has been the outstanding characteristic of secondary education in the present century.

As long ago as 1719 the problem which was to be the major issue in American education down to the present was already stated by a New England writer who announced that "the Plowman who raiseth grain is more serviceable than the Painter who draws only to please the eye. . . . When a people grows more numerous and part are sufficient to raise necessaries for the whole, then 'tis allowable and laudable that some should be employed in innocent arts more for ornaments than necessary. Any innocent business that gets an honest penny is better than idleness." The conflict between liberal education and the demands of practical life, which is clearly indicated in this statement, has continued down to the present time when the idea implicit in the statement has been rationalized into the theory that education must be "functional," or that necessaries must be assured first and creativity will follow.[1]

Benjamin Franklin in his *Proposal for an Academy*, written about thirty years after the comment on the plowman, endeavored to find a compromise between liberal and practical education. He wrote: "As to their studies, it would be well if they could be taught *everything* that is useful and *everything* that is ornamental.[2] But art is long, and their time is short. It is therefore proposed that they learn those things that are likely to be *most useful* and *most ornamental*; regard being had to the several professions for which they are intended." The grammar schools and colleges were not yet ready to adopt Franklin's suggestions, although academies were established to provide an education which might be both "ornamental and useful."

The last quarter of the eighteenth century, however, was to see the development of an American educational theory which was at once a protest against the European tradition and an attempt to adapt education to the needs of the young

Republic. The promise of a new social and political organization and an early vision of the great resources to be developed brought with them new ideas on education. Traditional education was to yield to the demands of the immediate and the practical; "aristocratic" or "monarchical" education was to be abandoned in favor of an education adapted to the "genius of the Republic"; education was to be adapted to the needs and abilities of a larger body of students. Except for modern pedagogical jargon, almost all the elements that make up the educational crisis of our times were already inherent in the effort to adjust education to the political, social, and economic needs of the day and to the divergent abilities and interests of the students. The majority of those who signed the Declaration of Independence may have been nurtured in the educational tradition of Western culture; some of their contemporaries and immediate descendants were already critical of that tradition. Their criticisms were based as much on political as on educational grounds. If their theories were not immediately put into practice, they served as a foundation for later development when the "common man" appeared on the American scene and challenged the "aristoi" of Jefferson's ideal, who a century later were to be denominated as "highbrows," or "brain trusts," or "eggheads."

Benjamin Rush was one of the first of the critics to enunciate the new trend. In 1786 he advocated a plan of education "accommodated to the present state of society, manners and government in the United States." "The business of education" had "acquired a new complexion by the independence of our country," and should be directed to exploring and applying the resources of the country. To study dead languages for four or five years is "to turn our backs upon a gold mine in order to amuse ourselves catching butterflies." New conditions of freedom and citizenship demanded a new type of education for "it is only by rendering knowledge universal, that a republican form of government can be preserved in

our country." Such an education would reject Latin and
Greek, which had been studied by the few and resulted, it
was alleged, in prejudice and bias, on the one hand, and, on
the other, failed to provide the training necessary to explore
and apply its resources. The traditional curriculum, because
it was "aristocratic" and "monarchical," was to be rejected
in favor of an education which would be "universal" and
"republican." Such a system "would greatly increase the
number of students in our colleges, and thereby extend the
benefits of education throughout every part of our country,"
and "the excellency of knowledge would then be obvious to
everybody, because it would be constantly applicable to some
of the necessary and useful purposes of life, and particularly
to the security and order of wise and just government."

Benjamin Rush did not stand alone in the views which he
expressed. Robert Coram in 1791 urged that "it was high time
to check that blind adherence to trans-Atlantic policy which
has so generally prevailed" and that schools should be "better
adapted to the present circumstances in America." Education
must promote equality and contribute to the preservation of
the new form of government, for "it is a shame, a scandal to
civilized society that part only of the citizens should be sent
to colleges and universities to learn to cheat the rest of their
liberties."

The same trend of thought was expressed by Noah Webster. The forefathers, he wrote, had "regarded colleges as the
best schools of wisdom and virtue," while "we consider them
as nurseries of inequality, the enemies of liberty." Writing on
*The Importance of Accommodating the Mode of Education
to the Form of Government* (1788), Webster urged that education must discard the monarchical pattern and be adapted
to the new republican form of government. Equality of educational opportunities must be provided, the curriculum should
include what is necessary for common intercourse, and "lads
should be directed to pursue those branches which are con-

nected more immediately with the business for which they are destined," for in his opinion "what is now called a liberal education disqualifies a man for business."

It is not surprising, therefore, that, when the American Philosophical Society offered a prize for an essay on "the best system of liberal education and literary instruction, adapted to the genius of the government of the United States," the writers who shared the award dilated on ideas which were already widely circulated. Samuel H. Smith in his *Remarks on Education* (1798) stressed the contribution which education might make to progressive improvement. "Will not the habit of reflection and progressive improvement continually devise new means of accomplishing a given object? Have not the powers of machinery already given a new creation to manufactures? And is not agriculture equally susceptible of improvement? . . . This progressive improvement would be promoted . . . by inspiring youth with a taste for, and an attachment to, science, so firm, that it should be almost impossible to eradicate it in the subsequent periods of life. . . . All science ought to derive its rank from utility. . . . Naked speculation is either unintelligible or uninteresting to the young mind. . . . From this plain view of the subject, it appears that in youth the addition of practical to theoretical knowledge would add to its charms."

Samuel Knox, the other successful competitor for the Society's prize, urged in his *Essay on Education* (1797) that liberal education should have "two great leading objects to which it should be adapted, the improvement of the mind, and the attainment of those arts on which the welfare, prosperity, and happiness of society depend." Hence "education ought to comprehend every science or branch of knowledge." There must be no class distinctions, since there can be no real equality without equality of educational opportunity. The function of education is to make man efficient in the tasks of daily life.[3]

The nineteenth century thus opened with an all-round attack on the tradition of liberal education, which was regarded as synonymous with "bookish learning." *The Columbian Phoenix or Boston Review* was launched in 1800 in an effort, as the editor wrote, to deny the charge of "indifference or rather apathy to genius and genuine literature which has been so often . . . represented as an inherent quality of Americans." An explanation of this charge was given by the Rev. Timothy Flint who wrote in 1826 that "the people" (of the Mississippi Valley) were "too busy, too much occupied in making farms and speculations to think of literature." Of the South, wrote Hugh Swinton Legaré in 1840, "a taste for literary studies (much more than any serious or continued application of them) stands very much in the way of a young man in the pursuits of an active life. It raises a presumption among worldly people that he can never become practical, and such a notion wherever it takes root in the public mind is beyond all comparison the most formidable obstacle a man of talents can encounter in such a state of society as ours. . . . Nothing is more perilous in America than to be too long learning and to get the name of bookish." Legaré, however, was but echoing that distinction between the intellectual and the man of affairs which Emerson had noted four years earlier in *The American Scholar.* "There goes in the world a notion that the scholar should be a recluse, a valetudinarian — as unfit for any handiwork or public labor as a penknife for an axe. The so-called 'practical men' sneer at speculative men, as if, because they speculate or *see*, they could do nothing." Then as now, the distinction was made between the highbrow and the lowbrow; but with this difference, that in Emerson's day it was still respectable to be a highbrow.

To all this must be added the new note injected into American culture by the rise of the common man, a note which is as marked and strident in education as in other aspects of that culture and which Carl Russell Fish so well summarized in the statement that "whereas Washington devoted his attention to bringing his gardens to perfection, men of the thirties and forties sought novelty rather than perfection" (*The Rise of the Common Man*, p. 105). The restlessness engendered by the realization of the unlimited potentialities of a country whose resources still remained to be developed had already been preceded by those theories of education which have been cited earlier, and demanded that education must be adapted to changing conditions.

MEETING THE NEEDS OF ALL PUPILS

The twentieth century thus opened with certain well-established principles. The first of these was a strong faith in education and the second a translation of this faith into the provision of equality of educational opportunities for all. The third principle which came to be accepted was that a new education must be devised to meet the needs of the large number of boys and girls for whom the academic curriculum was not suited. The differentiation of courses should, however, be provided within the comprehensive high school and not in separate schools. Efforts failed to adapt the curricula and courses to the individual differences of capacity and destination, while devoting attention to "constants," which all pupils were required to pursue. A new principle, which is now current and dominates all discussions of secondary education, emerged to the effect that education must be adapted to the needs, present and future, of all the pupils; in other words, the schools must provide an education for life adjustment. The assumption is that what is good for sixty per cent of the pupils attending high schools and, according to reports, deriving no benefit from this stay is also good for all pupils. This position was supported by the widely disseminated reports of the results of an eight-year study conducted under the sponsorship of the Progressive Education Association. These results were hailed as proof that graduates of thirty high schools, who were selected for the experiment, and who had been admitted to colleges on the recommendation of their schools and without having pursued the study of subjects required for entrance, had succeeded as well in their colleges as other students admitted on the conventional requirements.[4] The fact that these students had had good records in their schools, were submitted to a variety of tests, and ranked well in the Scholastic Aptitude Test was generally overlooked. The reports were used to bolster up the argument that it does not matter what a pupil studies in school so long as it is interesting and pertinent to his needs.

The evidence, on the actual situation in the high schools in general, that pupils failed to achieve a reasonable standard in what the schools undertook to teach was ignored.[5] Nor has sufficient attention been devoted to the qualifications of teachers many of whom are certificated as high-school teachers in general and not as competent in any specific fields, while others are expected to teach subjects that they have never themselves studied. The effect of the attempt to cater to pupils of every range of ability in the same school or in the same classes has been to neglect the pupils of superior ability. It is only recently that attention has been given to the problems arising from the neglect of the able and gifted students whose interests and abilities are sacrificed to standards suitable for the average.[6]

Programs for the reorganization of the high-school curriculum, adapted to the needs of all boys and girls and of contemporary society, began to be actively discussed in 1940, when the American Council on Education issued a pamphlet on *What the High Schools Ought to Teach*. The pamphlet had been prepared by a special committee for the American Youth Committee and other coöperating organizations. The committee based its recommendations on the fact that the number of pupils in high schools was increasing, were drawn from every level of society, and had a wide variety of plans

with respect to their future careers. Accordingly the traditional curriculum of studies was no longer suitable to meet
the needs of all pupils. As prospective citizens, however,
whose education would not be continued beyond the high
school they must all be made intelligent about the issues con-
fronting communities and the nation.

The secondary schools must, in the opinion of the committee, provide an education which is to be preparatory for
all contingencies of life. The use of the school years as a
preparation for self-education — *apprendre à apprendre* as
French educators put it — is ignored, and the promise and
prospects of adult education, whose paramount importance
in a democracy is beginning to be appreciated more than ever,
are not even mentioned. A few years before the traditional
curriculum had been rejected because its values were said to be
"deferred" and its replacement by a curriculum that possessed
immediate and affirmative value for the students was urged.
Education, it was then claimed, is life and not a preparation
for life. But even this theory seems now to be discarded and
the young adolescent is to be given a capital endowment,
while in secondary school, which will enable him as a member of the general populace to be intelligent about the issues
that confront communities and the nation. The assumption
seems to be made that the current issues which confront communities and the nation will always remain the same, or that
they can be anticipated, or, to adapt the Jacksonian idea, the
current issues are "so simple or admit of being made so simple
that any man can in a short time be master of them."

The committee considered the existing high-school program to be somewhat like patchwork and pointed to the need
of fundamental reforms. At the same time it admitted that to
make sweeping changes in order to improve the effectiveness
of all secondary education would be a mistake. The curriculum, however, did need reorganization to eliminate items that
were not adapted to the ability or the outlook on the future

of the majority of the pupils. The arguments are not clear, however, for two reasons: the first is that the high schools of the country had for some time been offering nearly three hundred courses, which should have provided sufficient flexibility for the selection of courses appropriate to the needs and abilities of all educable pupils. The second is that so little seems to have been achieved as a result of the innumerable commissions and committees which have studied the problems of secondary education in general and of secondary school subjects in particular during the past thirty years. The general tenor of the reports of these commissions and committees had been to stress individual differences and the provision in a sufficiently flexible array of subjects or programs adapted to the varying needs, interests, and abilities of the pupils, as well as to social and cultural changes.

The report, *What the High Schools Ought to Teach*, recommended that secondary education should be "adjusted to the needs of all young people"; those who have the ability to pursue the academic studies are apparently to be denied that opportunity. Greater attention is in fact given to pupils of low ability and to slow learners than to the able, because, one may infer, "it has been found that a great many pupils in these (secondary) schools have reading abilities of the fifth or even of the fourth grade level" (p. 12). That the progress of slow learners may be due to lack of interest in a particular subject or lack of proper motivation for study was admitted in the report, but it was believed that new devices could be found to stimulate the pupils to maximum endeavor. This, however, is the only suggestion in the report that pupil failures may possibly be attributed to inferior or incompetent teaching. Apart from the somewhat complacent and defeatist acceptance of the fact that the high-school curriculum must be adapted to the abilities of fourth- and fifth-grade readers, the report continued to follow the tendency, well-marked in all reports on secondary education in the past thirty years, to attribute the causes of pupil failure to the subjects of instruction rather to incompetent teaching.

The committee stressed the importance of books as means of education and deplored the attacks on bookish education. Only through ability to use books could pupils "take advantage independently and fully of the recorded experience of the race" (p. 14). The pupils were victims of "verbalism" and their minds were left untrained to interpret "what would be of great advantage if understood." The committee did not discuss further the place of the experiences of the race of the cultural heritage in a sound concept of education, but urged a widespread emphasis on library methods to cultivate individual taste and interests and to train pupils as "independent readers," even though many had only fourth-, fifth-, sixth-grade reading competence.

The committee suggested that the traditional subjects of the high school should be replaced by reading, work experience, and social studies in a program adjusted to the needs of the pupils and contemporary society. Work experience was recommended to meet a natural urge of youth to give expression to their energy and to learn to work steadily for eight hours a day. Such experience should not be looked upon as vocational training but as an important factor of general education. It was claimed pupils, through work experience and through handling tools, acquire insight into the nature of things and into their environment.

The social studies program which was recommended as one of the fundamentals of secondary education should include a long list of topics to replace some of the materials included in courses in history. Among the topics suggested as within the competence of young people to "form wise judgments based on knowledge of the facts," were the following: "housing, conservation of natural and human resources, community planning, coöperatives, pressure groups and their methods of influencing legislation, the stock ex-

change, corporations, labor organizations, the industries of
the nation, various forms of municipal government, governmental services such as those of the Departments of Agriculture, Commerce, and Labor, the origin and nature of money
and systems of exchange, international relations, consumers'
needs, and investments" (p. 23). To assess the value of this
program it is essential to remember the background against
which it was advocated — the inability of a large number of
high-school pupils to read.

The conventional subjects, it was urged, should be re-
examined and have injected in them "the same liberal spirit"
as in the new courses advocated. And so English and mathematics were to be reduced to fundamentals and foreign languages consumed too much time that could be better spent on
newer courses. Science courses were too often encyclopedic
and filled the memory with facts instead of stimulating pupils
to scientific thinking; how pupils could think without facts
was not suggested. In fine, the committee clearly considered
the traditional curriculum to be bookish, aristocratic, and
long, but sought to "democratize" education by teaching all
pupils to understand the perplexing problems of the day.

THE TEST OF WAR NEEDS

Two years after the publication of *What The High Schools
Ought to Teach*, the urgent needs of the armed forces for
trained personnel provided the opportunity to assess the
validity of the criticisms of the educational tradition which
had become stereotyped. A letter issued on January 15, 1943,
by the Chief of Naval Personnel, Rear Admiral Randall
Jacobs to "The High School Teachers of the Nation" contained the following paragraph: "In general, high schools
should continue to improve instruction in such basic courses
as physics, mathematics, the other sciences, and English.
These subjects are fundamental to advanced instruction in
the technical phases of naval activities and should not be

supplanted by courses in aeronautics, radio, navigation, and other similar specialized subjects."

Along the same lines Admiral Chester W. Nimitz had reported two years earlier that in an examination for entrance into the Naval Officers Training Corps sixty-eight per cent of 4,200 candidates who were college freshmen, were unable to pass the arithmetic reasoning test, sixty-two per cent failed the whole test which included arithmetical combinations, vocabulary, and spatial relations. Only ten per cent had already taken trigonometry in high school, and twenty-three per cent had had more than one and a half years of mathematics. Similar results were found in other examinations of candidates for appointment as officers in the Navy.

An inquiry conducted by the *New York Times* in 1942 had revealed widespread ignorance and much misinformation about American history among 7,000 students in thirty-six colleges to whom the test was given. Even if it were admitted that the test was open to criticism, the results were disturbing, especially as it was later shown that the teaching of history was required in thirty-eight states and was customarily taught in all other states. The American Historical Association, the Mississippi Valley Historical Association, and the National Council for the Social Studies appointed a committee to survey the situation. The committee found that the teaching of history was not neglected in the schools; instead it attributed the insufficiency of the results to the inadequate preparation of teachers and poor methods of instruction. More important, in view of the trend against subjects as such, was the forthright statement of the committee on the value of teaching history as a subject and not as an incidental part of some amalgam or an integrated course. The committee expressed its belief that "there are values in the study of systematic and organized bodies of materials, for the understanding of society and its problems the study of the slow evolution of institutions and nations is necessary. The careful study of history will result in an understanding of chronology, continuity, cause and effect, and of trends, forces, and movements." In *The Social Studies Look Beyond the War* (1944), prepared by the Advisory Commission on Postwar Policy of the National Council for the Social Studies stress was also placed on the importance of the historical approach to understand postwar problems.[7]

UNIVERSAL SECONDARY EDUCATION

The committee which had prepared the report on *What The High Schools Ought to Teach* concluded with the statement that "some central agency seems, however, to be necessary to bring the issues of curriculum revision more prominently to the attention of the general public and of teachers. There has long been some recognition of the problems with which this report deals and there have been promising innovations in the curriculum introduced at various centers. What is required now is a vigorous effort on the part of central agencies . . . and energetic classroom teachers to produce the changes in secondary school programs that are long overdue." One such agency, the Educational Policies Commission of the National Education Association, issued a report in 1944 on *Education for* ALL *American Youth*. In the opening chapter, "The History that Should Not Happen," which purports to consist of "quotations that may possibly be found in the concluding pages of some standard history of education *published some twenty years from now*," the statement is made that the schools were unprepared for the war but showed ability to react to a national wartime crisis, and that "no one seems to have noted that the (familiar prewar) pattern, too, was shattered beyond repair; that the end of the war was the end of an epoch to which there could be no return, in education or in any other aspect of life" (p. 4).

The committee responsible for the preparation of the report on *What the High Schools Ought to Teach* had concluded its work in 1940, before the outbreak of the war, and could not at that time anticipate the difficulties of the Army, Navy, and other services in securing personnel adequately equipped in mathematics, sciences, and foreign languages — parts of "the familiar prewar pattern of education." The Educational Policies Commission, however, must have been fully informed of these difficulties as well as of the widespread fear lest the Army and Navy educational programs would result in an overemphasis on vocational and technical training, a fear which at the college level resulted in the appointment of local and national committees to discuss measures to preserve the ideal of a liberal education. Looking backward from 1964 the Educational Policies Commission claimed that "the tremendous pressure of the traditional educational program" was responsible for the difficulties in education in the postwar years, forgetting that the traditional pattern of education began to be shattered some thirty years earlier, when the quantitative measure of education — the units, credits, points system — was adopted and any subject began to be considered as of equal value with any other subject taught for the same length of time, thus resulting in the abandonment of any concept of subject values, and when the doctrine of formal discipline was assumed to have been "exploded." The consequences for a long time had, in fact, been the absence of any pattern, whether in high schools or colleges, other than the completion of the requisite number of units or points. In the 1952 edition of the *Education for* ALL *American Youth*, however, it was stated that "A good general education is the best preparation for service in war as well as for service in peace." Mathematics and sciences, mechanics and electronic communication (the mother-tongue), and foreign languages (for pupils with aptitudes for them) are included in a general education.[8]

The commission recommended, in the latest as well as in the original edition, the organization of curricula and courses

which could take into consideration the major types of educationally significant differences among American youth, the
significant characteristics common to them all, and the provision of educational programs to meet the common needs of
all youth and the special needs of each individual. "Every
youth in these United States — regardless of sex, economic
status, geographic location, or race — should experience a
broad and balanced education which will (1) equip him to
enter an occupation suited to his abilities and offering reasonable opportunity for personal growth and social usefulness;
(2) prepare him to assume the full responsibilities of American citizenship; (3) give him a fair chance to exercise his right
to the pursuit of happiness; (4) stimulate intellectual curi-
osity, engender satisfaction in intellectual achievement, and
cultivate the ability to think rationally; and (5) help him to
develop an appreciation of the ethical values which should
undergird all life in a democratic society." [9]

The education of the majority of youth is expected to
continue from the seventh to the fourteenth grade, the last
two years in the community institutes or community colleges
which would be provided more generally in the future. In
Grades VII, VIII, and IX, the period of common secondary
education, a common program will be provided to help the
pupil "to grow in knowledge and understanding of the world
in which he lives; in ability to think clearly and to express
himself intelligently in speech and writing; in his mastery of
scientific facts and mathematical processes; and in his capacity
to assume responsibilities, to direct his own affairs, and to
work and live coöperatively with other people." [10] Through
a wide range of experiences in "intellectual, occupational,
and recreational fields" the pupil will have "a broad base for
the choices of the interests which later he will follow more
intensively." In the later grades the curriculum, organized
into three fields — occupations, intellectual pursuits, and
recreational interests — will be differentiated to suit the needs

of each individual, while the common fields — education in the responsibilities and privileges of citizenship, family living, health, and understanding and appreciation of the cultural heritage — will be continued. The cultural heritage is nowhere further defined nor are any designated fields or sequences to be followed as prerequisites for admission to higher educational institutions until the student enters the community institutes. Teachers will be expected to suggest "tailor-made" learning experiences adapted to the interests and abilities of each pupil in the common integrated courses which will form the bulk of the curriculum. Through the integrated courses pupils will acquire such knowledge as they may need of history, language and literature, sciences and mathematics with the provision of remedial work for the backward and of extra time for the able pupils to pursue their special interests in these fields. What would happen if a pupil fails to recognize the need of these subjects is not indicated.

The traditional organization of the curriculum by subjects is to be discarded in favor of "areas of learning" and the course itself is to be an adventure for all — pupils and teachers. The "areas of learning" proposed for Grades X to XIV of a rural high school and community institute are as follows: [11]

Preparation for Occupations

Study and practice related to occupational preparation (including, work in science, mathematics, social studies, English, or foreign language preparatory to advanced study in college or university, as well as education for agricultural, mechanical, commercial, and homemaking occupations)

Education for Civic Competence

Community studies and civic projects, extending into larger areas (including "The World of Work")

Historical study of "Man's Efforts to Achieve Freedom and Security"

Investigation of current political, economic, and social problems; study of their historical backgrounds; and civic projects

Personal Development
Family life, health, and mental hygiene (including the domestic, personal, and health aspects of consumer economics)
Recreational and leisure-time interests, including physical education

Understanding and appreciation of the cultural heritage
"The Scientific View of the World and of Man"
Historical study of "Man's Efforts to Achieve Freedom and Security"
Literature and the arts
Elective studies or individual projects, or (in Grades X–XII) remedial instruction in English or mathematics, if needed

Apparently the so-called subjects are to be taught incidentally as the need for them may arise. According to the time distribution given for the program, about thirteen per cent of the total number periods for the five years are to be devoted to "understanding and appreciation of the cultural heritage" and then only in the first three years. And even if a pupil feels disposed to devote all the time assigned throughout the course to elective studies or individual projects in this "area of learning," the time allotment would still be only twenty-five per cent of the total.

The "areas of learning" are designed with an emphasis "on the present living of youth, on the improvement of community life, and on such practical matters as competence in occupations, citizenship, and family living." These areas were more generally referred to as education for life adjustment as will be pointed out later. These, it is assumed, will "develop the discipline of sustained intellectual effort needed for success in advanced academic and professional study." The argument is as follows: "For one thing, most of a student's learning at Farmville (where the rural high school and community institute are located) is directly *related to his purposes.* The student *wants* to do something, either as an individual or as a member of a group. He applies himself diligently to learn the things needed to do what he wants to do, and thereby develops habits of application and industry." [12] This is the progressive theory that children and youth can embark on an educational exploration or adventure without any idea of their destination or a preliminary study of the map. The teachers are to serve as guides and counselors and to participate with their students in organizing the content of the "areas of learning." In the end the student is presumably to emerge with such knowledge, ideas, and values as are related and suited to his purposes and wants.

The same general principle of integrated "areas of learning" in terms of vocational and civic needs, adapted in turn to individual interests and abilities are to be followed in the urban high school and community institute. Here the program consists of the following "areas of learning": [13]

Individual Interests

Elected by the student, under guidance, in fields of avocational, cultural, or intellectual interest

Vocational Preparation

Includes education for industrial, commercial, homemaking, service, and other occupations leading to employment, apprenticeship, or homemaking at the end of Grade XII, XIII, or XIV; education for technical and semiprofessional occupations in community institute; and the study of sciences, mathematics, social studies, literature, and foreign languages in preparation for advanced study in community institute, college, or university. May include a period of productive work under employment conditions, supervised by the school staff. Related to the study of economics and industrial and labor relations in "Common Learnings"

Science

Methods, principles, and facts needed by all students

Common Learnings

A continuous course for all, planned to help students grow in competence as citizens of the community and the nation; in understanding of economic processes and of their roles as producers and consumers; in coöperative living in family, school, and community; in appreciation of literature and the arts; and in use of the English language. Guidance of individual students is a chief responsibility of "Common Learnings" teachers

Health and Physical Education
Includes instruction in personal health and hygiene; health examinations and follow-up; games, sports, and other activities to promote physical fitness. Related to study of community health in "Common Learnings"

In the discussion of the curriculum there appears to be some uncertainty as to values. On one page the commission is of the opinion that the first of "the imperative educational needs" of youth is to be equipped to earn a living in a useful occupation; on the next page the statement is made that education in family living is according to some teachers "second to nothing in importance"; and a few pages later education in community competence is declared by the commission to be "paramount in importance."

The possible objection that the traditional subjects of the secondary school curriculum have been neglected could be met by the statement that the common learnings would include English language, literature, history and social studies "though possibly in unaccustomed settings," while systematic bodies of knowledge or subjects required for college entrance could be acquired in the ample time left in the total program. The programs of each year's work would be planned in advance, and within those outlines, pupils and teachers would plan and organize their own learning, an intellectual effort in its own right.

There is a confusion in the commission's report between training and education — training in and for the immediately contemporary problems of living and education for life and for self-direction. The school years are to be devoted to acquiring all the equipment of knowledge and information and habits and attitudes that the students will need through adult life rather than acquiring a body of ideas, principles, and values which will not only inform that knowledge but will also cultivate interest to pursue it further. One of the major blocks of the course is to be devoted to preparation for a useful occupation, despite the admission that most workers are now engaged in routine, repetitive activities and that most schools cannot afford to provide specialized and expensive equipment for vocational training.

In discussing principles of teacher education and selection the commission warns against "the influence of members of college and university faculties who are unacquainted with the needs of public schools and who apparently believe that specialized training in subject matter alone is adequate to prepare a young man or woman to teach in a secondary school." It therefore recommends that "every teacher should comprehend the purposes of public education in a democratic society," "prepared to assume his own obligations as a citizen" and understanding "how the school may serve as an agency for developing civic responsibility." Professionally educated to understand boys and girls, and familiar with scientific information regarding child development and the psychology of learning "every teacher should have both a liberal education and thorough preparation in the field which he expects to teach. Specialization alone is not enough, for in the secondary school of today, the competent teacher must be able to see and teach the relationship of his particular subjects to the whole of education and the whole of life." [14] A fuller and more detailed definition of the meaning of a liberal education, to which the commission refers, would have been desirable. It would also have helped to clarify the function and place of the teacher with a "thorough preparation in the field which he expects to teach" in a course made up of occupational, social, and recreational studies which are stressed throughout the report.

In the historical retrospect, "The History that Must Be Written," a chapter omitted from the 1952 edition, no further reference is made either to a liberal education or to preparation in a special field. Instead, the changes which are expected to have taken place since 1940 are as follows: "First, there was a great strengthening of instruction in educational psychology, individual differences, human relations, adolescent psychology, human growth and development, and educational guidance and counseling. . . . Second, the study and teaching of school and community relations and of educational sociology were greatly strengthened. Prospective teachers were given more close firsthand contacts with other community institutions as well as with the schools. . . . Third, the expansion of the school program in the fields of guidance and vocational training has resulted in a parallel expansion of the program for preparing teachers in these fields." [15] There is apparent a discrepancy between the principles of teacher education as defined in one place and the historian's anticipation of what is more likely to happen.

Very few changes were made in the edition of *Education for* ALL *American Youth* which appeared in 1952. It was noted that "the secondary school of today is a new school and a still growing one" and that "the functions of the school since the close of the first world war have changed and expanded greatly." Changes are needed because many adolescents who should be attending school are not doing so, there is a large percentage of "drop-outs," and "a very large number of youth in secondary school are not getting an education fully suited to their abilities, interests, and needs." These facts are put forward as the bases for the drastic changes that are suggested as the ideal. The last chapter of this edition is devoted to an account of the ways in which "Education for All American Youth Moves Forward." The main lines of development are: (1) guidance and student adjustment activities; (2) vocational education developments; (3) community and school relations; (4) recent curriculum adjustments; and (5) developments in statewide secondary education.

For purposes of the present account, the results of the discussions on recent curriculum adjustments in urban secondary schools are revealing. There were agreements on the following points: "(1) The youth entering high school today represent so great a variety of background and ability that teachers should expect them to show a reading competence extending from fourth grade through twelfth grade standards. (2) Many high school students' abilities are such that they will never be capable of going beyond sixth, seventh, or eighth grade reading levels. (3) Teachers cannot justify a school curriculum designed to meet the needs of only the superior ranges of ability; every youth has a right to expect and experience a high-school education adjusted to his needs and the development of his interests and capacities. (4) Standards of student performance will be satisfactory if students are working with materials adapted to their abilities. (5) All teachers are responsible for helping students read and interpret textbooks and other materials essential to the mastery of the courses taught. (6) All youth who work to capacity should receive full credit, regardless of the level at which they learn. Proper guidance will prevent them from entering courses beyond their capacities." [16]

The report of the Educational Policies Commission on *Education for* ALL *American Youth* was popularized in a summary published by the National Association of Secondary School Principals under the title *Planning for American Youth* (1944). The pamphlet proposed the creation of a Commission on Postwar Education to consist of representative elementary and secondary school principals and teachers, laymen representing citizens and vocational advisory committees, and directors of research, curriculum, and instruction. The absence of any provision for a representative of college education is noticeable. The major attention was apparently to be given to the needs of the nonacademic students; those students who have the ability and interest to engage in academic studies would follow the courses adapted to the "imperative needs" of all youth and devote such time as could be spared from the "common learnings" to academic subjects in preparation for entrance to college.

EDUCATION FOR LIFE ADJUSTMENT

This trend was re-enforced following a conference of leaders in vocational education held in Chicago in 1945. At this conference Dr. Charles A. Prosser, director of Dunwoody Institute, Minneapolis, Minnesota, offered the following resolution, which has since then always been referred to as the "Prosser Resolution."

It is the belief of this conference that with the aid of this report in final form, the vocational school of a community will be able better to prepare 20 percent of its youth of secondary school age for entrance upon desirable skilled occupations; and that the high school will continue to prepare 20 percent of its students for entrance to college. We do not believe that the remaining 60 percent of our youth of secondary school age will receive the life adjustment training they need and to which they are entitled as American citizens — unless and until the administrators of public education with the assistance of the vocational education leaders formulate a comparable program for this group.

We, therefore, request the U.S. Commissioner of Education and the Assistant Commissioner for Vocational Education to call at some early date a conference or a series of regional conferences between an equal number of representatives of general and of vocational education — to consider this problem and to take such initial steps as may be found advisable for its solution.[17]

The resolution was obviously concerned with the failure to provide an education suitable to meet the needs of the pupils. The result of the deliberations of the National Commission for the Education of Youth [18] was to lead to the adoption of the principle that all American youth had the same "imperative needs" and that all should have the same common education for life adjustment, irrespective of destination. In other words, it was decided that an education that was good for sixty per cent would be good for the other forty per cent despite differences in aptitudes, abilities, and interests.

Accordingly, what was desirable was a union of vocational [19] and general education in a common core to provide a life-adjustment education to meet the needs of all pupils. Such a curriculum, it was argued, would help to hold pupils longer in school, would avoid discrimination by denominating one course as suitable for nonacademic pupils and another as good for the academically and technically able. A common life-adjustment education would hold the American people together and avoid a division into groups. Such a program would help to democratize education, and, with the new methods of learning by experience and doing, the progresses of learning through group action and pupil participation in planning would also become democratic instead of authoritarian and dictatorial as they had been in the past.

The high school, it was frequently reiterated, had been restrained by a tradition of education dominated by academic college-entrance requirements. The time had come when it must develop its own philosophy of education in terms of objectives directly related to the needs of its pupils and its community. The school must prepare for effective living and not be concerned primarily with specialization. Experiments in the Eight-Year Study and with mature veterans, who had not completed their high-school education, had shown that the courses required for college entrance were neither essential nor important for success in college studies. Further, the effectiveness of an education cannot be evaluated in terms of knowledge acquired or of mastery of abstract concepts in logically organized subject-matter courses, but in terms of the development of skills, habits, attitudes, understandings, and appreciations.

The "imperative needs" of youth were popularized by the Educational Policies Commission in *Education for ALL American Youth* and by the National Association of Secondary-School Principles in its Bulletin for March 1947. They are on examination an expanded version of the *Cardinal Principles of Secondary Education* (1918). The imperative educational needs of youth were defined as follows: [20]

1. All youth need to develop salable skills and those understandings and attitudes that make the worker an intelligent and productive participant in economic life. To this end, most youth need supervised work experience as well as education in the skills and knowledge of their occupations.

2. All youth need to develop and maintain good health and physical fitness.

3. All youth need to understand the rights and duties of the citizen of a democratic society, and to be diligent and competent in the performance of their obligations as members of the community and citizens of the state and nation.

4. All youth need to understand the significance of the family for the individual and society and the conditions conducive to successful family life.

5. All youth need to know how to purchase and use goods and services intelligently, understanding both the values received by the consumer and the economic consequences of their acts.

6. All youth need to understand the methods of science, the influence of science on human life, and the main scientific facts concerning the nature of the world and of man.

7. All youth need opportunities to develop their capacities to appreciate beauty in literature, art, music, and nature.

8. All youth need to be able to use their leisure time well and to budget it wisely, balancing activities that yield satisfactions to the individual with those that are socially useful.

9. All youth need to develop respect for other persons, to grow in their insight into ethical values and principles, and to be able to live and work cooperatively with others.

10. All youth need to grow in their ability to think rationally, to express their thoughts clearly, and to read and listen with understanding.

In essence, the needs appear in the following paragraphs of *Life Adjustment Education for Every Youth*.[21] "The school is one of the important institutions which exercise educational influence, and as such it must assume its full share of responsibility for the behavior of adults. Contemplation of current affairs in American life must convince even those who are most optimistic about the future that all possible means should be used to strengthen the function, both within and without. There are needs for improving the health of our people and for conserving our natural resources. There are needs for strengthening the family and stabilizing our practices for ethical living. There are needs for defining our foreign policy and governing ourselves in more responsible fashion. There are needs for placing and keeping our economic machinery in balance and for making more recreative our use of leisure time.

"It is apparent that American adults are sorely tried in their efforts to solve the problems forced upon them by the problems of modern living. Upon those who have a faith that schools can and do make a contribution to intelligent adult behavior, there rests an obligation for improving the schools."

To meet the life-adjustment needs the following objectives must be stressed and subject matter introduced as needed, but the curriculum must be centered in the needs of youth. Attention must be devoted to "guidance and pupil personnel services; ethical and moral living; citizenship; home and family life; self-realization and use of leisure; health; consumer education; tools of learning; work experience, occupational adjustment, and competence; and administrative, financial, and organizational arrangements in the school." No place is provided for knowledge or information in a curriculum "designed and adjusted as to content, scope, and sequence, so as to be practical, real, and definitely related to youth, his life, his work, and the society in which he lives." The reason for this absence of knowledge is that the basis is "a philosophy of education which places life values above acquisition of knowledge." The values are reached by modern methods of personal experience, group discussion, and coöperative thinking.

The blame for the deficiencies of the high schools was placed in recent educational literature, as they have been for about half a century, on college-entrance requirements which are alleged to have stood in the way of the reconstruction of the curriculum and its adaptation to the needs of what has become the majority of the pupils in the high schools. Thus in the Office of Education Bulletin, *Life Adjustment Education for Every Youth*, the statement is made that "the retention of the college-dominated curriculum is often responsible for the high-school's failure to serve adequately a large proportion of its population. Especially is this true of the small high school where the necessity of meeting accreditation standards and the pressure from the patrons of the high school who demand the offering of certain subjects, conspire to maintain the dominance of the college-preparatory curriculum at the expense of the great percentage of the pupils who will not go to college." [22] The high schools should become autonomous and independent in determining the credits to be granted. Since, it is argued, research has proved that a successful college career does not depend on the preparatory studies that pupils have had, all pupils should have the benefit of a life-adjustment education. This would eliminate the segregation of pupils according to abilities and destination and preparation for college could be postponed to the last year of school and admission to college be based on a new scheme of measuring ability to do college work.

A later report of the second commission on Life-Adjustment Education appointed in 1951 — *A Look Ahead in Secondary Education: Education for Life Adjustment* (Office of Education, Bulletin 1954, No. 4), repeats much of what had already been written on the subject and adds some information on the development of state programs to indicate the progress made along the new lines for "redirecting, reorganizing, and retooling education." The report refers to the variations in the plans and programs to implement the ideal of life adjustment and indirectly confirms the continuance of the practice of adding to the patchwork that makes up the curriculum of high schools.

The fact that the ideal neither grows out of practice nor out of demands of teachers and administrators, despite the insistence on the democratic process, is suggested in the following sentences: "Even without the interruption of a world war, there would have been a long, hard task of translating the findings of these and other studies into a working program for the secondary schools. In the first place, there was a staggering job of learning, to be undertaken by teachers and administrators. The future program seemed to demand a teacher in each classroom, laboratory, and shop who would be a combination psychiatrist, social scientist, scientist, and an individual of considerable culture, who was also a man or woman of action. Some educators were inclined to believe that a blueprint for a Utopian Secondary School had been proposed which could only be operated by teachers of rare genius." [23]

By this time it seems to have been forgotten that what is now looked upon as a Utopian Secondary School was first proposed for sixty per cent of the pupils who derive no advantage from the existing high-school curriculum. The "staggering job" is facilitated by denying the desirability of ability grouping for "Ability grouping and similar administrative arrangements are no longer embraced as panaceas for solving problems of individual differences. Small schools find the problem of scheduling of different groups impossible. In large schools it is comparatively easy to organize groups on the basis of general intelligence and reading achievement but much more difficult when such additional factors as socio-economic background, emotional development, and rates of physical maturation are considered." [24] The administrative and sociological argument, therefore, seems to point to mass education and "a colorless mean," which is no solution to the problem that has been in the forefront of American secondary education for about four decades — how to implement educationally the ideal of equality of opportunity.

Thus the historic conflict, which began with Benjamin Franklin's opposition of the ornamental and the useful, and later of the academic and practical or functional, seems to be settled in favor of the latter in recent theories on secondary education. In 1893 the Committee of Ten had declared that an education good for those pupils planning to go to college was good as a preparation for others of the minority of American youth enrolled in the high schools. That statement read as follows: "The secondary schools of the United States, taken as a whole do not exist for the purpose of preparing boys and girls for colleges. Only an insignificant percentage of the graduates of these schools go to colleges or scientific schools. Their main function is to prepare for the duties of life that small proportion of all the children in the country — a proportion small in number, but very important to the welfare of the nation — who show themselves able to profit by an education prolonged to the eighteenth year, and whose parents are able to support them while they remain in school." There was nothing in this statement that committed the schools to give the same curriculum to a larger number. But today that formula has been reversed and it is maintained that an education that is good for the sixty per cent (including pupils with fourth-, fifth-, and sixth-grade reading competence) who do not go to college is good for those who will continue their education beyond the high school. In other words, the abilities of "a proportion small but very important to the welfare of the nation" are to be stunted in favor of the majority who also need an education but of a different kind for their duties of life as "citizens, home-makers, and workers." The ideal is reminiscent of a recent popular slogan of equalitarianism in Australia: "Cut down the tall poppies."

The general trend that seems at present to dominate the discussions of the purposes of secondary education, is to plan the program of life-adjustment education on the basis of the first of the duties of the high schools as defined by Dr. Thomas

H. Briggs: "The first duty of the school is to teach people to do better the desirable things that they are likely to do anyway." The second duty, which from the point of view of education rather than training is more important, has generally been ignored, perhaps because of its possible association with traditional values of liberal education. That second "duty of the school is to reveal higher activities and to make them both desired and to a maximum extent possible." To attempt to carry out this duty would mean a subject-matter approach which is rejected by the "modern" school. According to its proponents, the program of a modern school should be organized along the lines of problems of vital and immediate concern to the pupils rather than in terms of remote and dead past.

Few educational innovations have had the benefit of such extravagant propaganda as the programs for the education of all American youth and for life-adjustment education. The advocates, however, are regretfully forced to admit that there are difficulties in the way of bringing about a revolutionary change in the high schools. Paradoxically, it is stated those difficulties are created by teachers, pupils, parents, and the public as well as teacher-education institutions. Teachers prepared in the liberal arts and teachers colleges find it "difficult to turn aside from respectable content and to venture with materials which are scarce and often poorly organized." [25] The content — college entrance requirements — has acquired prestige, and the teachers have a jealous regard for that prestige and their own status. Both elements — status and prestige — make teachers conventional and wedded to routine practices. Principals and administrators, fearful for their jobs, refrain from encouraging innovations that might lay them open to criticism. The pupils, on their side, prefer the daily round of assignments and memorizing from textbooks the content on which they may be tested instead of participating in planning and exercising initiative and origi-

nality. Parents and the public are devoted to traditional standards of educational values and prefer courses whose results
are measurable to those which seem vague and opportunist.
The teacher-education institutions are conventional and ad-
here to a program consisting of compartmentalized subjects
and fail to prepare teachers to carry on an experience-, problem-centered education. Finally, college entrance requirements stand in the way of the fullest development of the
interests and abilities of talented pupils because of their
rigidity, a point which on many counts is not accurate but
chiefly because there has been a general relaxation of this
rigidity until in many institutions the only requirement left
is English.[26]

The chief vehicle for conducting an experience-centered
(or pupil- or problem-centered) curriculum is the "core curriculum," which has in recent years acquired much notoriety.
The definition of the core curriculum varies; it may mean the
correlation of related subjects or the integration of subjects,
or an interdisciplinary approach drawing on whatever content is called for in discussing a problem. In any case, its basic
purpose is to break down compartmentalization of the program into subjects and to devote longer blocks of time to a
discussion than is usual in the traditional time schedule. It
aims, when experience centered, to promote coöperation of
teachers, planning by teachers and pupils, and the use of as
great a variety of resources, excursions, and visits to institutions to reduce the bookish character of traditional learning
methods.

SECONDARY EDUCATION AT MID-CENTURY

For about three decades the predominant feature in the
literature on secondary education has been the critical attack
on the courses offered, scepticism about the value of academic
and particularly of preparatory courses for college entrance,
and an emphasis, on the one hand, on the needs of all pupils

attending high schools, and, on the other, on the importance
of training to meet the pressure of the rapid cultural changes.
The conditions have, however, been too unstable to permit
of the introduction of wholesale changes along the lines described in the preceding pages. The number of pupils increased rapidly, partly because of the depression which
limited the opportunities for employment of youth, and partly
because the age of compulsory school attendance was raised
to sixteen or even to eighteen in some states. Because the enrollments increased rapidly it became impossible to secure
an adequate supply of teachers, and this situation was rendered
more difficult by the exodus of teachers from the profession
during World War II. A factor that was still more important
was the unfavorable attitude of teachers, pupils, parents, and
public to revolutionary innovations which would not only
change the pattern of secondary education, but would en-
danger the preservation of the traditional concept. This unfavorable disposition was, as pointed out earlier, regretfully
admitted by the proponents of the radical changes.

The effects of a theory that emphasized freedom and abandoned discipline made themselves felt in the high schools
more than in the elementary schools particularly strikingly
in the postwar years. Boys and girls in their adolescent years,
who in another era could have been put to work or appren-
ticed, were now compelled by the attendance laws to go to
school and had become unemployable in any but blind-alley
occupations. The general relaxations of those social influences
— the family, the church, clubs, and other youth organizations — and of other disciplinary influences left the adolescents too frequently without any controls at a time when they
most needed guidance. Scholastically, many high-school students could find little to interest them in the curriculum
offerings, despite their expansion. The disciplinary problem
became acute and in some cities certain schools were recognized as difficult and appointments in them were, if possible,

avoided. Teachers were not only unable to do their work of instruction but were at the mercy of students who deliberately made their tasks difficult for them. The situation is not unlike that in elementary schools when compulsory attendance was introduced, but at that time at least corporal punishment was a deterrent. The situation today is different, partly because of a change in social conditions which are now recognized to be the prime causes of the postwar increase in juvenile delinquency. While it is possible to exaggerate the influence of the delinquents when in school, there is no doubt that they create a problem which is not conducive to the successful conduct of classroom instruction.

The present situation is, therefore, confused. To read the literature on secondary education, whether by individual writers or by leading organizations, such as the National Education Association's Educational Policies Commission or the Life Adjustment Education Commission, would leave the impression that a revolutionary change was already beginning to take place. The varied practices in the high schools would, however, dispel that impression. Most generally the high-school programs are either organized into demarcated courses or are made up ("tailor-made") for each pupil by a teacher or guidance counselor who selects available subjects he considers suitable to his abilities. However, certain subjects are expected to be studied by all pupils; these are English and social studies. According to the report of a second commission on Life-Adjustment Education (*A Look Ahead in Secondary Education*, p. 80), "separate curricula for college preparation, vocational agriculture, and commercial work, which filled the school handbooks in years past, are tending to disappear. In the larger schools, pupils no longer pursue a long sequence of courses which must be completed when they elect one curriculum or another. Each pupil, with the help of teachers, parents, and counselors, selects a program of studies from the list of required and elective subjects which takes into account his personal interests, needs, aptitudes, and plans for the future. Flexibility, freedom, and a recognition of individual differences have been substituted for rigid patterns of courses designed to achieve standards of academic or vocational specialization."

According to a report [27] by the U.S. Office of Education, 274 subjects were offered in all the high schools of the country taken together. This is to be interpreted as meaning that under each subject a number of one-year courses were offered. Thus social studies included: United States history, world history, state history, ancient and/or medieval history, world geography, American geography, community civics, occupations, orientation, Latin-American history, modern European history, American government, problems of democracy, international relations, economics, sociology, and consumer education, and, more unusually, industrial history and geography, Negro history, English history, and history of the Orient.

Under science were reported: general science, biology, botany, physiology, zoology, earth science, aeronautics, physical science, chemistry, physics, fundamentals of electricity, radio including electronics, conservation, and, in some places, nature study, applied chemistry, applied physics, fundamentals of mechanics, applied biology including social biology, metallurgy, and laboratory techniques.

The largest enrollments were in the subjects required in most states — health, safety, and physical education. Of the foreign languages Spanish had the largest enrollments with Latin a close second, while French was taken by fifty per cent and German by ten per cent of the numbers in Spanish courses. In all languages, however, the mortality was high, the majority dropping out after two years in a course.

The 274 courses include academic and practical subjects. The former are the subjects of a traditional secondary education; the latter include industrial arts, which are nonvocational, and vocational trade and industrial courses, commercial courses, home economics, and agriculture. Vocational preparation in trade and industry, in home economics and in agriculture has been encouraged by Federal grants under the Smith-Hughes Act (1917) and supplementary acts. The general practice is to include some industrial or practical work in the academic programs and some general studies in the vocational programs.

Out of the 274 courses various programs may be made up. The programs that are most generally found are the academic, business or commercial, general education, and various types of vocational programs. The only point that is definite about all the programs is that in order to graduate fifteen or sixteen points must be completed in the four years. Even the program for those intending to go to college is no longer as definite and specific in its requirements as it once was. Colleges have tended to relax their requirements and the only subject that is still required is English, although pupils would in general be advised to take a foreign language, mathematics and science, and history. For admission, colleges generally take into consideration the quality of the high-school record, recommendation of the principal of the high school attended, personal qualifications, and showing on an aptitude test, generally the Scholastic Aptitude Test of the College Entrance Examination Board. The effects of this relaxation of entrance requirements may be reflected in the statistics of mortality in colleges where from forty to sixty per cent of the students who enter fail to reach graduation.

The full effects of the curricular developments were not recognized until the shortage of trained personnel in languages and sciences was realized during World War II and in the postwar years when the need of trained manpower in physics, chemistry, and engineering. In a booklet, *Teachers for Tomorrow*, issued in 1955 by the Fund for the Advancement of Education, it was reported that forty-six per cent of the high schools offered no foreign languages, twenty-four per cent no geometry, and twenty-three per cent neither physics nor chemistry. A few months later, Admiral Lewis L. Strauss, chairman of the Atomic Energy Commission reported that fifty-three per cent of the schools did not teach geometry, and in the same issue of *The New York Times* (December 8, 1955), Dr. John R. Dunning, dean of the School of Engineering, Columbia University, was reported to have stated in an address to the American Institute of Consulting Engineers that "no high school anywhere in our country has even one-half the Russian requirements in mathematics, sciences, physics, and chemistry." This situation is not due to inferior ability on the part of the nation's youth, but to a certain leveling down and a shortage of well-prepared teachers, as well as to the notion that the classification of pupils according to ability is undemocratic. The issue is not only a curricular one, but of social and national import as seems to be realized in the movement to find and help gifted and talented students, which is discussed later in this chapter.

DIFFERENTIATION OF COURSES AND QUALITY OF EDUCATION

The United States, in undertaking to provide educational opportunities beyond the elementary schools for all boys and girls, has embarked on a social experiment for which there is no precedent in any other country. Indeed, the provision of some form of postprimary education for all up to the age of fifteen or sixteen has only been undertaken recently in a few countries. The word "experiment" has been used advisedly, for American secondary education, as may have been gathered from the preceding pages, is still in an experimental state. A solution that will satisfy all who recognize and believe that the provision of equality of educational opportunities for all youth is an essential feature of the democratic ideal is not easy to find. Faith in education for all is based on a conviction on the worth and dignity of all — citizens and potential citizens — and on the belief that education contributes to the well-being of the individual and the progressive welfare of society. But the danger to be avoided in implementing the ideas is the confusion of equality with identity. The results in practice of attempting to subject all pupils to the same curriculum and an extensive literature on individual differences in abilities, interests, and needs are a sufficient warning against attempting to give all pupils the same education — whether it is academic and general or practical and vocational.

Undoubtedly, it is the function of secondary schools as a part of the common school system to provide all pupils, irrespective of their destination, with a common foundation for mutual understanding coöperation, and with common objects of social allegiance, but it would be too much to expect that divergences can be avoided by giving all pupils the same program and teaching all by the same methods. It is questionable whether instruction based on the pupils' experience would not involve a considerable waste of valuable time. There are differences of environment — social, economic, and cultural — differences of intellectual capacity, differences of interests, and ultimately occupational differences that cannot be avoided or side-tracked. Ignoring such variations, to which differences in the ability and competence of the teachers themselves may be added, has resulted in the tendency which "is always to strike a somewhat colorless mean, too fast for the slow, too slow for the fast. The ideal is a system which shall be as fair to the fast as to the slow, to the hand-minded as to the book-minded, but which, while meeting the separate needs of each, shall yet foster that fellow-feeling between human being and human being which is the deepest root of democracy." [28]

This neglect or inability to cope adequately with this aspect of the problem has led, on the one side, to a vast expansion of the curriculum with two hundred seventy-four courses, all assumed to have the same educational value, or, on the other, to an attempt to give all the same basic instruction by the same methods on the Jacksonian assumption that "the duties of any public office are so simple or admit of being made so simple that any man can in a short time be master of them." This assumption has not only been applied to political issues but to all contingencies of life and for all pupils — the able as well as those with fourth, fifth, or sixth grade reading competence. An educational program, originally intended for the sixty per cent who apparently derive no benefit from their stay in high school, is now assumed to be equally good for those planning and able to continue their education beyond the high school.

The fundamental problem continues to be not one of differentiating between those pupils who are likely to go to college and those who will not, but one of finding the right education for the right pupil and not discriminating against any group. At present, by the catering to the average or producing "a somewhat colorless mean," the slow and able or talented pupils are not receiving the education that is their due. Not only are the facts of nature and nurture ignored in most proposals for reform, but the needs neither of society nor of the individual pupil receive the consideration that is their due. The loss to society through the neglect of the able pupil, who is himself in danger of wasting his ability as a result, is incalculable.

For this the scholars and specialists must bear some of the blame. The committees that considered problems of secondary education before 1900 were made up in about equal numbers of representatives of the schools and of academic subjects in liberal-arts colleges. The latter have had no representation on general committees that have considered the reform or reorganization of secondary education in this century. The gap between those concerned with the two levels of education — secondary and higher — became wider as the mid-century approached. The specialists in science were the

first to awaken to the importance of looking to the future by
providing the right education for potential scientists at an
early age. In the colleges scholars became disturbed about the
future of the humanities but paid little attention to what was
going on in the secondary schools; the exception is the
Harvard University Committee's Report on *General Education in a Free Society*. Science and technology were able to
attract students because of the spectacular developments in
these fields.

In 1953, at the annual meeting of the American Council
of Learned Societies (ACLS), the secretaries of twenty-five
constituent societies, felt that an interest in American education in general must be shown by scholars, and after a conference a committee on the Relation of Learned Societies to
American Education was appointed. This committee was to
draw up a plan to study the proper relations of the constituent
societies to American education "with especial reference to
the preparation of teachers, certification of teachers for secondary schools, junior colleges, and four-year colleges, and
to explore the possibilities of cooperation with learned societies not associated with the ACLS." A number of constituent societies have committees of their own to consider
the matter, as, for example, the American Historical Association and the Modern Language Association.

Dr. James Bryant Conant, former president of Harvard
University, put his finger on the problem of educating able
students in the following statement: "For there is no doubt
that the use of our public schools consciously or uncon-
sciously to keep our society 'democratic' and fluid presents
us with an educational dilemma. The more we try to employ
the instrument of universal education to offset those forces
of social stratification inherent in family life, the more we
jeopardize the training of certain types of individuals. In
particular, we tend to overlook the especially gifted youth.
We neither find him early enough, nor guide him properly,

nor educate him adequately in our high schools." Accordingly, Dr. Conant expressed the wish that "some organization identified the public mind with concern for *all* American youth would take some dramatic action to demonstrate a vigorous interest in the gifted boy or girl. This would serve as an encouragement to all teachers. The schools would be stimulated in a direction which in some quarters has been rather spurned as being undemocratic and old-fashioned. A National Commission for the Identification of Talented Youth has been suggested by one group of educators." [29]

In 1950, the Educational Policies Commission, of which Dr. Conant was then a member, published a report on *The Education of the Gifted*, a subject neglected in its earlier report on *Education for* ALL *American Youth*. In the later report by the Commission the following statements appear: "The democratic ideal can be most fully attained when every individual has opportunity for educational experiences commensurate with his abilities and for vocational responsibilities commensurate with his qualifications." After describing the importance of "the basic sciences of man and nature," the statement is made that "specialization must be built on a broad foundation. The implications for the education of potential leaders in the sciences and their application are clear; their study of mathematics and the basic sciences must be extensive; and it must start early, for they will need their later college and post-college years for professional training and other kinds of specialized work." How important the education of able and talented boys and girls is for the nation must be gathered from the following passage: "To the extent that the American people fail to face reality by recognizing that the superior abilities of gifted individuals do in fact exist, they tend to impair the full development and function of those abilities, thus denying to themselves a measure of the potential benefits." [30]

In *Science, the Endless Frontier*, which was published in

1945 as a report by Dr. Vannevar Bush to the President of the United States, a strong plea is made by one of the committees — the Committee on Discovery and Development of Scientific Talent with Dr. Henry Allen Moe as chairman — for the early selection of pupils of talent not only in the sciences but in other areas of intellectual endeavor. The plea is made in the interests not only of the advancement of knowledge but also of national progress. Two pertinent passages may be cited as illustration of the argument: "The intelligence of the citizenry is a national resource which transcends in importance all other national resources. To be effective that intelligence must be trained. The evidence shows that many young people of high intelligence fail to get the training of which they are capable. The reasons for that failure are chiefly economic and geographical and can be remedied."

Again: "As citizens, as good citizens, we therefore think that we must have in mind while examining the question before us — the discovery and development of scientific talent — the needs of the whole national welfare. We could not suggest to you a program which would syphon into science and technology a disproportionately large share of the nation's highest abilities, without doing harm to the nation, nor, indeed, without crippling science. The very fruits of science become available only through enterprise, industry, and wisdom on the part of others as well as scientists. Science cannot live by and unto itself alone. . . Plans for the discovery and development of scientific talent must be related to the other needs of society for high ability; science, in the words of the man in the street, must not, and must not try to, hog it all." [31]

The need of discovering and developing able or gifted or talented pupils has been widely recognized. More recently the importance of doing so has impressed itself on lay and professional leaders in science, technology, and engineering because of reports of rapid expansion in the number of practitioners in these areas in Soviet Russia. But it is also widely recognized that programs for the education of scientists and engineers will be inadequate and unbalanced unless potential leaders have some acquaintance also with the humanities and social sciences, or, in other words, an understanding of human values and human behavior. This, no doubt, is what the Moe Committee had in mind in the reference to the need of "enterprise, industry, and wisdom on the part of others as well as scientists." In an age, when science and technology are commanding so much of the public attention, a proper balance is needed between the values inherent in the sciences and the values that can be found in the humanities and the social sciences. In the search for talent there is also a great need for discovering those young people with ability in the humanities, in languages, and in the social sciences.

It is accordingly the national needs, not only for highly trained technological and scientific manpower but also for manpower trained in other areas of intellectual leadership, that are outstanding and so far as current high school education is concerned are ignored in theory and inadequately met in practice. In the words of the Director of the Educational Testing Service, Dr. Henry Chauncey, "The manpower resources we fail to develop may cost us our survival. What can we do to prevent the waste? The systematic use of tests to identify our most talented youth and help ensure they receive the right kind of education that will enable them to make the best use of their capabilities would seem to be one important and very specific action that can be taken." [32]

Before the question of organization of secondary education is discussed, there is the question whether such talent can be identified. Dr. Conant's statement which antedated Dr. Chauncey's implies that such identification is possible: "There is considerable evidence to indicate that linguistic and mathematical ability can be recognized in the early high school years;

musical talent, of course, makes itself apparent much earlier. We have long been accustomed to discovering the boy or girl in the artistic field and we are providing more and more for the education of such talent within the school. But relatively little is done along parallel lines for those who have comparable talent in languages and mathematics. Yet how much society has to gain by the early recognition of such people and their adequate education!" [33]

The logic of these discussions would appear to point to the provision of some special organization for the education of the gifted or talented pupils. Although there exist separate technical high schools, separate vocational schools, and high schools of science and of music and art, any proposal to create special schools for the gifted would meet with widespread opposition. The reasons that would be alleged against such an organization would be that it is undemocratic, discriminatory, and divisive. Although there is ample evidence, to which references have already been made, that at best the high schools can only achieve mediocrity and neglect the able and the slow pupils, and although evidence can be advanced to the effect that schools cannot in fact overcome the social, economic, and cultural differences among the pupils since they reflect the existence of such differences in their environmental background, the notion still persists that school instruction can promote solidarity. [34]

There seems to be inherent, in the objection to separate provision for able students as undemocratic, a concept of democracy that smacks of the herd. There is also a misconception of the concept of equality of opportunity, the danger of which has already been mentioned. But contiguity and mass organization are no guarantee of democracy nor is identity of treatment the same as equality. The ideals of democracy or, to use a more popular phrase, the ways of democracy are not acquired by "adjusting" all pupils to the same pattern. Respect for others and for their rights, the assumption of

duties and responsibilities which lead to service and coöperation, the development of a pattern of conduct consistent with
democracy — all these can be learned and acquired in ways
that are more varied than they can be in a comprehensive
school. More important is the increased opportunity that can
be provided in a separate school or division of a school for
pupils to stretch their abilities as far as they can go without
the frustration that comes on the one hand from being kept
back or on the other from being measured against the more
able.

There remains the serious problem of the small high school
with some two hundred pupils and a handful of teachers.
The needs of the gifted can hardly be met except by instruction in small numbers which may be beyond the means of
the small community. An alternative may be found in the
concentration of able pupils in schools serving a number of
small schools. The essential point, however, is that the problem of able pupils in small schools be recognized. It may be
that here and there a teacher may be found, who, like the
dominie in Scottish schools, recognizes ability and is sufficiently competent to stimulate, encourage, and assist it to the
fullest development of which it is capable. Such teachers exist
and some have been publicly identified.

The problem of secondary education is likely to become
more serious in the next decade as a result of higher birth rate
during and after World War II. It is expected that the enrollments will reach as high as ten million pupils by 1961, and
that the enrollments in colleges will show a corresponding
increase. The fundamental issue will, indeed, remain the same:
How to define equality of educational opportunity in such
a way that each pupil receives the education and training
appropriate to his abilities and interests. Another aspect of
this issue is how those pupils who have the ability to work
with ideas and abstract symbols are to be prevented from
having that ability atrophy under a policy of adjustment or
education for *all* American youth.

Two characteristics of American civilization — and those not the most desirable — seem to have influenced the thinking both of those who interpret the education of youth predominantly in terms of "common learnings" which inevitably lead to instruction in a common pattern, and the advocates of life adjustment education who, disregarding the premise on which their movement was initiated, would level out the education of all to a program deemed, without evidence, to be appropriate for the sixty per cent who derive no benefit from the existing programs and the majority of whom do not have the reading ability required for the new program. The first of these influences is the traditional aversion to academic studies as aristocratic or for the privileged or nonpractical. The second influence is the more recently growing pressure to conformity, a pressure under which those of academic ability are regarded as eccentric, anomic, or maladjusted. To these another influence may be added, that of an industrialized and mechanized civilization, which favors mass production, on one hand, and, on the other, looks upon education as a piece of machinery that can be "redirected, reorganized, and retooled."

The critic of the trends described in this chapter runs the risk of being charged with being undemocratic and unsympathetic to the ideal of providing equality of educational opportunities. Apart from the fact that it would be patently absurd for anyone today to question the ideal which most democracies are seeking to attain, there can be no doubt about the sincerity of those who are sceptical of an interpretation of equality which deprives any group of the education appropriate to the abilities that it can demonstrate and who doubt whether herdmindedness or adjustment is a symbol of equality. The instruments for discovering abilities are available and will continue to be improved, but a realistic interpretation of the results and of the education to which they point is still needed. It is still more needed if the quality of education is not to be overwhelmed by the quantity.

There is another approach which the proponents of the new secondary education fail to make. This approach involves more than following the guidance of the immediate and the contemporary conditions and paying homage to needs and changing conditions. It involves a study of the history of culture and civilization to discover the mainsprings of human progress. It will be found that the culture and civilization of the world have been advanced by ideas and by the "know-what" and not by the progress of the machine. To accept the second view is to accept the notion of the economic determination of man's progress. To accept the first is to encourage those who show promise of ability to work with ideas and to give them an education that will bring that promise to fruition by starting as early as possible. And that can be achieved not by "retooling" the curriculum but by securing teachers whose sympathetic insight into the intellectual rights of the pupil is as deep as their culture. The problem is as much a social as it is an individual one.

The American people are justifiably proud of their "know-how," but it would be unfortunate if this pride were allowed to conceal the fact that the "know-how" would be impossible to achieve without the quiet contribution of those who "know what" and push forward the frontiers of knowledge. No one has better described the principle inherent in this than the late Dr. Edward L. Thorndike when in a discussion of the distribution of education he said: "Doubtless great ability will often manage to get an education outside the schools or to get along without it, but those who can do so much for the world with so little are the very ones who should be given more. In the wars we are incessantly waging against disease, misery, depravity, injustice, and ugliness, we should not provide our best marksmen with the poorest weapons nor ask our bravest to fight with their naked hands."

CHAPTER V

The Teaching Profession

RAISING THE STANDARDS OF THE PROFESSION

Criticisms of the low standards of teacher preparation and qualifications began to be heard in the last decades of the nineteenth century. A movement to raise these standards and to place teaching on a professional basis began on the eve of the twentieth century. It was actively promoted by such educational leaders as G. Stanley Hall, Charles W. Eliot, and Nicholas Murray Butler, and by the National Educational Association, which was assuming a position of great influence as the most important organization of teachers. The association appointed three committees in the last decade of the nineteenth century, whose purpose was to recommend improvements needed in elementary and secondary education. Another committee on College Entrance Requirements was appointed to consider the relations between secondary and higher education. The reports of all these committees emphasized the importance of raising the standards of the preparation of teachers.

The movement to raise standards implied a change from a brief preservice course devoted to imparting the skills of the trade to relatively immature and inadequately educated young men and women, who predominated, to a course of preparation brought ultimately up to a level similar to that required for entrance to other professions like law, engineering, or medicine. Other factors had to intervene before these standards could be reached even on paper. A change of attitude toward and a new understanding of the work of the teacher had to be brought about before progress could be made in advancing both the standards of preparation and the status of teachers.

There prevailed, in fact, the notion that anyone could teach, that teachers were born and not made, and that the only preparation needed by a teacher was mastery of subject matter. The quantum of knowledge to be imparted at a particular stage in a pupil's schooling was parceled out by grades by the administrative authorities; the details were prescribed or were provided in textbooks; pupils were expected to memorize those details and "recite" them in class; teachers were supervised to see that they carried out the prescriptions and pupils were examined to see how well they had mastered them. What the teacher could not accomplish by skill or personality, could be achieved by rigorous discipline, including the use of corporal punishment.

The standards of admission to the occupation were so low that they almost seemed to bear out the notion that anybody could become a teacher. And they were low because licenses to teach were administered locally and granted on inadequate educational standards, varied in values from temporary to life certificates, and were normally not interchangeable. Appointments were generally for a year at a time with the right of local school boards to "hire and fire." Since, for the greater part of the nineteenth century, teaching was one of the few occupations that women could enter and since women constituted a majority, there was a rapid turnover and a stable profession could not be built up. To the turnover among women teachers must be added the turnover among the men who took up teaching as a temporary occupation until they found something better. To quote Professor William C. Bagley, "teaching was not a profession but a procession," and it continued to be such until there was an improvement in standards of preparation, conditions, of tenure and salaries, and status in general. In the middle of the twentieth century, as will appear later in this chapter, despite improvements in standards of preparation, the economic status of teachers was not so sufficiently attractive that teachers could resist the lure of better remunerated activities.

Before 1900, the majority of teachers for the elementary schools were trained in high schools or normal schools, which in most cases had still to give their students a general secondary education as well as training for their work. Although in New York State in 1890 and in Massachusetts in 1894 normal schools began to require the completion of a high-school course for admission, the supply of high schools throughout the country was still too small for such a requirement to become generalized. Normal schools continued for a long time to be considered on a lower level than institutions that required high school graduation for admission. Nor was there before 1900 much professional content available, if higher standards of professional preparation were to be attained. Techniques of teaching and school and classroom management constituted almost all the material that could be taught. The educational literature in the latter part of the nineteenth century was described by Nicholas Murray Butler in 1899 as "on too low an intellectual plane to meet the needs of the day."

<h2 style="text-align:center">THE PROFESSIONAL STUDY OF EDUCATION</h2>

Such literature may have been on too low an intellectual plane, but there was a certain amount of scepticism abroad in the last decade of the nineteenth century about the possibility at all of developing a scholarly literature in the field of education. The generally prevailing view was expressed in 1891 by Josiah Royce, and has been quoted earlier (see

p. 94). When Royce expressed this view, however, the movement to recognize education as a subject of university study had already begun. A chair in education had been established at the University of Michigan in 1879; G. Stanley Hall gave courses in psychology and education at Johns Hopkins University after his appointment to lecture in philosophy in 1881; Paul Hanus became professor of education at Harvard University in 1891, and in 1898, Teachers College, founded ten years earlier as the New York College for the Training of Teachers, became a department of Columbia University. At a meeting of the National Educational Association held in 1891 Nicholas Murray Butler declared that the university had a duty to the teaching profession and that "university chairs of pedagogy were being established. Thought is being devoted to the question. The movement is a great one and is destined to grow."

The study of education until the turn of the century still consisted of borrowings from psychology and philosophy, somewhat in the spirit suggested by Josiah Royce. But developments in an entirely different direction toward an independent science of education were already foreshadowed in the shift of interest from "pure" psychology to the observation and recording of the tendencies of the child in physical and mental growth. As early as 1882, G. Stanley Hall had established a laboratory at Johns Hopkins University for the study of child development and of adolescence, a study which became one of the major activities of Clark University of which Hall became president in 1889. At about this time, Francis W. Parker directed attention to the importance of recording and using as a guide in education the spontaneous tendencies of the child. Out of these early beginnings there developed a change in the theory of education which was later to lead to the establishment of the child-centered school.

A change in the same direction was forecast by the attack on formalism in education initiated by John Dewey in 1894 and by his experimental school at the University of Chicago, and his emphasis not only on relating school practice to the developing interests of the child but also on the social aim of education in a democracy. Some time was to elapse before the ideas advanced by Dewey were to become a major influence in American education.

In the interval, the improvement of teaching methods, selection of content, and a stronger emphasis on the moral purposes of education were fostered by the importation of the theory of Herbart by Americans who had studied education in Germany, among whom the leading Herbartians were Charles DeGarmo and Charles and Frank McMurry. The Hebartian movement not only provided a basis for study but it displaced the traditional faculty psychology by another concept of mind and thus opened up another important area of study of the factors involved in the process of learning. The leading figures in the development of a new psychology were William James and Edward L. Thorndike.

When the twentieth century opened the foundations for an expanding area of study had been laid in education. It gradually broadened out from "pedagogy" or principles, history, and the practice of education with a little psychology until it embraced every possible approach to the education of human beings from infancy through life and in every type of institution — primary, secondary, higher, vocational, and adult. It included also the study of the contributions of sociology and anthropology to education, the administration and financing of education, the organization of schools and school systems, and tests and measurements of intelligence and achievement. In the opinion expressed in 1900 by James E. Russell, Dean of Teachers College, Columbia University, "university departments of education have as their special function the investigation of educational foundations, the tional methods, and the application of educational principles. interpretation of educational ideals, the invention of educa-

The science of education . . . needs to be developed and made over to fit modern conditions."

Two other important needs had to be met before the preparation and status of teachers could move to a higher plane. The first was the adequate provision throughout the country of secondary schools without which normal schools still had to provide a general and professional education to young and immature students with little more than an elementary education or two years of high school. The provision of high schools depended upon the growth of areas large enough to support them. The growing industrialization of the country led at the beginning of the century to aggregations of population in villages, towns, and cities and a change from a predominantly agricultural to an industrial economy, from predominantly rural to urban conditions. Urbanization and prosperity made it possible not only to provide more and better schools in general, but also to expand the opportunities for education beyond the elementary schools. At the same time the enlargement of school systems demanded a type of organization and administration different from that which prevailed in the nineteenth century. One of the chief tasks undertaken by the new administrators was to "sell education" to the public, to convince them of the value of education for social, civic, and economic progress. To that end the public was expected to provide the means for better school buildings and for recruiting better prepared and better paid teachers. The stage was thus set for raising the standards of admission to normal schools and of the work of the normal schools themselves.

A change in the granting of teaching certificates also played an important part in helping to raise the standards for the employment of teachers. Between 1900 and 1910 examinations for certificates by local officials were gradually replaced by examinations conducted by state boards or state departments of education, but more generally by the award of certificates by such bodies to graduates of normal schools provided that certain professional subjects had been included in the courses. A similar procedure was followed in certificating graduates of liberal arts colleges who intended to teach in secondary schools. The requirements set by state authorities for certificates exercised a strong influence on the organization of the work of the normal schools and colleges.

NORMAL SCHOOLS BECOME TEACHERS COLLEGES

For the greater part of the first twenty years of the twentieth century the normal school was the chief institution for the training of teachers for elementary schools; courses in high schools were still provided in a few states for the training of teachers for rural schools. The normal schools sought in the two-year courses offered by them to provide academic studies, professional work, which included a review of the materials that the elementary-school teacher would be expected to teach, and observation and practice teaching in the practice or training school under the supervision of critic teachers.

Despite a quantitative rise in standards in terms of admission and years of study, the normal schools did not escape criticism. Generally they were criticized on two grounds — that the academic work was of low grade and that too much time was devoted to techniques and methods of instruction instead of content. An effort to raise the level of the academic courses by providing a body of "professionalized subject matter" in place of review courses did not altogether meet the criticisms that were made. How much that failure was due to misunderstanding of the meaning of "professionalized subject matter" and how much to a continued tendency on the part of those concerned with college and university education to regard professional training with scepticism cannot be determined. This tendency was of the same character as that noted by G. Stanley Hall in 1891 which he described as "the disastrous chasm between the university and the schools. On the one side of it we find the Philistinism of the common school teacher; on the other the exclusiveness of the university man."

It was in part the resentment caused by the criticisms, and in part a desire to have the right to train high-school teachers, in part to facilitate the passage of their graduates to liberal arts colleges, that prompted the normal schools to consider a further improvement in standards. The expansion of the professional literature of education and the accumulation of research studies may also have contributed to this. But the factor that was more important than any of these was a gradual change in the concept of the function of the teacher. This began to change slowly from imparting a definite quantum of knowledge and information to a mass of pupils to a better understanding of each pupil as an individual, different from others in ability and personality and coming from a background distinct from that of the others in the class. There began also a movement to change the character of the classroom from a place where the pupils sat still and passively learned what was imparted to them by the teacher or recited what they memorized from a textbook to a place where pupils were actively engaged in cultivating their interests with the teacher as a guide. The old type of discipline was in theory discarded in favor of responsible freedom, just as fixed seats and desks were replaced by movable furniture. All this placed new demands upon the teacher. Other responsibilities were to be added later as the social function of the school as a constructive agency of society began to be emphasized.

Accordingly, the normal schools gradually began to assume the title of "teachers colleges" partly to place themselves on the same level as liberal arts colleges and partly to be able to offer degrees at the end of a four-year course and so attract candidates who wished to become teachers in secondary schools. It was thus possible for teachers colleges to offer a general education and so compete with liberal arts colleges.

Even before World War II a few teachers colleges dropped the word "teachers" from their names and became "state colleges," if they were publicly maintained institutions. This practice was followed by many other teachers colleges after the war in an effort to attract veterans who were given opportunities to continue their education under the G.I. Bill of Rights. To meet the needs of students who did not intend to enter the teaching profession a variety of new courses were added.

Certification requirements have been defined and administered by each state with the result that there is a great variety of standards which has militated against reciprocity. The courses in teachers colleges in preparation for such certificates may be two, three, or four years in length for elementary school teachers, and normally four or five years for secondary-school teachers. In 1953 the bachelor's degree of professional preparation was required for the lowest regular elementary school teaching certificate in twenty-five states, but in some of them provisional or temporary certificates could still be granted below this standard. Four states (Arizona, California, New York, and Washington) required five years of preparation, that is, one year beyond the bachelor's degree, for high-school teaching certificates in academic subjects, while forty states required the bachelor's degree for the lowest high-school teaching certificates, and in three states only two years of preparation were required. In eighteen states blanket high-school teaching certificates are granted without the endorsement of any specific academic subject or subjects, their assignment being left to the appointing authority and the approval of some accrediting organization.[1]

The state requirements may be exceeded by local authorities, as they are in the larger cities. There are no national standards, nor perhaps would they be desirable. About twenty years ago a privately administered scheme to conduct National Teacher Examinations was established with the purpose primarily of testing the general education of candidates for teaching positions. The examinations do not take the place of the requirements for certificates but may be in addition to such certificates or to local requirements. Higher types of certificates are granted on the basis of this examination. The National Teacher Examination is now conducted by the Educational Testing Service in Princeton, N.J.

Insofar as national standards can be defined, it is done in the case of teachers colleges as it is in the case of high schools and liberal arts colleges through voluntary bodies, state, regional, or national. Normal schools have been accredited locally or regionally for their general or academic work. From 1923 to 1954 the teachers colleges continued to be accredited in this way, but for the professional work the accrediting was conducted under standards and policies of the American Association of Colleges for Teacher Education. In 1954 the accrediting responsibilities of the AACTE were turned over to the newly established National Council for Accreditation of Teacher Education, which adopted the standards of the AACTE. The standards deal with the objectives and organization of a college for teacher education; with admission, selection, guidance and placement of students; with the preparation and teaching load of the faculty; with curriculum-instructional patterns; with professional laboratory experiences; with library and financial support; with appointment, academic freedom and tenure; and with standards for advanced professional programs.

CURRICULUM OF TEACHERS COLLEGES

The general trend in the organization of the curriculum of a four-year teachers college, an ideal not yet reached in all states, is to provide for the students' general education, for specialization in one or several allied subjects, and for professional competence through the study of the appropriate professional subjects and practice or "laboratory" experience in schools attached to the colleges or in local schools. The scheme of organization varies but three forms can be found. In the first arrangement, the course is equally divided into two years for general and two years for professional studies including specialization. In the second arrangement, general and professional studies are taught side by side through the four years. In the third pattern, some professional studies are begun in the first two years alongside of general education with concentration on them in third and fourth years.

The interpretation of what constitutes "general education" varies but the purpose is clear. It is to counteract the tendency toward specialization, to meet the criticism that the emphasis in teacher education is too technical, and above all to give the future teachers a broad educational background useful for their personal development, for their understanding of the world in which they live, and to enrich their professional activity. General education also serves to give teachers a cultural background which they enjoy in common with other educated persons. It comprises a program of study which includes English language and literature, social sciences, natural sciences, and humanities with a tendency toward integration of several branches under one of these titles.[2] Specialization in one or more subjects that a student plans to teach may include a more intensive study of one of these branches. The change is expressed in the replacement of the term "training of teachers" by the term "education" or "preparation of teachers," the old term connoting the imparting of routine skills and the new implying the study of principles to be used by a broadly educated teacher.

The professional studies, which have been subjected to frequent attacks from critics of normal schools and teachers colleges, include the history and principles (or philosophy) of education, educational psychology, classroom (or school) management, general and special methods of teaching, and observation and teaching practice. Some of these subjects may be divided, for example, into history of elementary or of secondary education, or tests and measurement, or psychology of childhood or of adolescence. Another general course, "social foundations" or "school and society" may include some history, principles, and sociology.

In 1952 a new scheme of teacher education was started in Arkansas and then extended to other centers with the help of grants from the Ford Fund for the Advancement of Education. To meet the criticisms of lack of general education and overemphasis on professional studies the new scheme provides for the appointment of graduates of liberal arts colleges as interns in schools where they are to combine learning the art of teaching on the job with courses or seminars on education to discuss problems that may be encountered by the student. Considerable opposition to the experiment was expressed by those concerned with the preparation of teachers.

"THE ACADEMIC CIVIL WAR"

Considerable progress has obviously been made in the past thirty years since normal schools became teachers colleges. The development has not, however, escaped the traditional criticism that they lack the standards of a liberal education and devote too much time to professional studies. Undoubtedly, the expansion in number and scope of these studies as a major activity in the advanced study of education and the wave of experimentation both in research and in practice have had a strong influence on teachers colleges intended for the preservice training of teachers. Another cause for this emphasis is a certain desire to professionalize teaching by basing it on a foundation of somewhat esoteric subjects, a cause which may also explain the cult of a special jargon which has been termed "pedagese." This raised the old question, already propounded by Josiah Royce more than half a century earlier, whether teaching is an art or a science. There is no doubt that what has been contributed to a better knowledge of the psychological and physiological growth and development of the child and the adolescent, of individual differences of ability, of interests, and of the learning process has been of pre-eminent value for the improvement of the art of education. Equally important has been the inclusion in a philosophical consideration of the interrelation of education with society and the culture patterns of the environment. But how much of such material the cadet-teacher should study and how much a clear interpretation would contribute more effectively to better teaching has not been considered. This question does not exclude the desirability of expanding the bounds of our knowledge of education in its many facets. But to attempt to impart such knowledge to those about to enter the teaching career would be like including the latest and still unverified contributions of an advanced medical research institute in a medical school course.

Nevertheless, much of the criticism of teacher education from the outside is due to ignorance of the actual distribution of time between general and professional studies as well as of the inherent problems of teaching. Those who claim that he who knows his subject can teach are apt to forget that even in such a case the master of a subject acquires his skill as a teacher through experience with pupils or students and often at their expense. On the other hand, those who emphasize professional preparation forget that those are three data in the educative process. Sir John Adams, a professor of education with experience in teaching Scottish, English, and American students, once summarized that process in the simple statement that it was directed "to teaching John X," that is, that it involves a knowledge of subject matter (X), of the pupil (John), and of the art of instruction. The critics of systems of teacher education stress the subject matter; those who emphasize professional studies today stress the child on the principle, to use a phrase which first appeared in English educational literature, that there has been a shift of emphasis from the subject to the child. At the same time, in America there has been a shift in the emphasis of the art of teaching from imparting knowledge and information to pupils to putting them in "a learning situation" where they learn by their own "experiencing." [3]

Another broadside attack on educators is to the effect that their theories have produced the anti-intellectualism that now prevails. The emphasis on learning by experience, on doing rather than on thinking, on the "how" rather than the "what," on emotional rather than intellectual development, and on life-adjustment education — the slogans of the period since World War I — have produced a great deal of busy-ness in education but in the long run few results intellectually. The stress on the contemporaneous, current social problems has failed to develop an understanding of the past that has produced them and have not succeeded in developing any better understanding or appreciation of the meaning of democracy, which their proponents profess to be their goal.

Whether the charge that anti-intellectualism is a product of the schools or whether the practical has not always been more appreciated than the intellectual in American culture need not be discussed here. [4] The scholars who are the chief among the critics have themselves been the products of American educational institutions. There is a tendency to forget, in the flush of pride over the nation's achievement in providing equality of educational opportunities, that schools previously attended by a select minority have been thrown open to pupils whose I.Q. ranges from that of a moron to the highest possible figure. The academically able students are less numerous than the less able who lack the intellectual ability needed to pursue a traditional academic course and who come from a less favorable background, social and cultural. It is in the interests of the average and particularly of those who are not likely to proceed to college that many of the changes went on in the curriculum reconstruction of the past generation. It is only since the end of World War II that serious attention has been devoted to the education of the able and gifted student. In the current situation the major attention is being devoted to the search for promising students in the sciences; the need of gifted students in the humanities and social sciences is equally urgent in the interests of the nation. Given a choice between Jeffersonian and Jacksonian principles, educators in the main have chosen the latter. The unfortunate part of the proceeding is that they have sought to rationalize on the value of the latest as the best not only for the majority but also for the minority. And to that end they have tended to adjust their definition of democracy.

The objecting scholars cannot be blamed for criticism of the exaggerated claims put forward on "scientific" and "social" grounds for the unacademic and anti-intellectualistic trend. On the other hand, these scholars have not made any effort to recognize the problem or to suggest methods of putting the Jeffersonian principle into operation. They have on the whole remained aloof without even coming to the protection and preservation, until very recently, of the subjects that they themselves profess.

Referring to this "academic civil war" between scholars and educators, President James Bryant Conant in a lecture delivered at Teachers College, Columbia University, in 1944 suggested a truce between the combatants on the two sides of the academic fence.[5] While he deplored the lack of knowledge, understanding and sympathy on the part of scholars, he might also have viewed with regret a certain prejudice among educators against scholars not unlike that which Emerson discussed more than a century ago. That scholars are beginning to see the need of showing an interest in public education has already been mentioned in Chapter I.[6] Any understanding or *rapprochement* that may result from the report, prepared by Professors Howard Mumford Jones, Francis Keppel, and Robert Ulich for the Committee on the

Teaching Profession of the American Academy of Arts and Sciences and submitted to the Committee on the Relation of Learned Societies to American Education, will redound to the advantage of teacher education practices and the public schools of the nation. The promotion of a better understanding between the academic and pedagogical or professional faculties was recommended by the President's Committee on Higher Education in vol. III, p. 61, of its report published in 1947.

The "academic civil war" also arises out of the shift of the educational pendulum to an extreme that is not realized by the scholars, nor endorsed by all educators. The public and the scholars tend to be misled by the vociferous claims made for the latest innovation. Nevertheless, if changes in the work of the classroom teacher are limited to the contributions that have come from educational psychologists and a realistic study of the movements in American culture, it is clear that the responsibilities of the teacher have changed considerably. He is no longer responsible for imparting lessons with the aid of a textbook to pupils regarded as an undifferentiated mass. To teach successfully he must be familiar with each pupil as an individual and with a cultural background which has to be supplemented or enriched. He must find out what a pupil can do and help him do it in accordance with his ability. He is expected to put his pupils in the way of learning by their own efforts rather than memorizing what they are told in class or learn from a textbook. He must be able to relate what the pupils learn to their environment and to the society in which they live in order to ascertain whether they are able to understand the meanings of what they learn. Whether the teacher shall also be a social engineer to help the pupils to reform society, or a mental and physical hygienist, counselor and adviser, functions which are sometimes suggested as the teacher's responsibilities (see quotation on p. 3), is a question open to debate. If the major aim of helping pupils to understand the world in which they live and which is constantly expanding in range and scope of meaning as they grow and develop — intellectually, emotionally, morally and aesthetically — is accepted, common ground can be discovered to restore the unity of the teaching profession at all levels.

THE STATUS OF TEACHERS

Despite the advances made in the preparation, the status of teachers has not greatly improved in the twentieth century. Teachers still bear the onus of a bad tradition inherited from the preceding century, when the emergence of women into one of the few occupations that was then considered respectable for the sex exposed them to the gibes of the cartoonist and the ridicule of young and old. The "schoolmarm" may have disappeared, but her stereotype remains. Nor were the conditions of service conducive to building up esteem and respect, for the requirements for admission to the trade were low, the turnover was great because the occupation was a temporary period of waiting until the opportunity for marriage arrived, and the salaries were commensurate with the training and the duration of service.

The general education and professional preparation of teachers have increased in time and quantity, although their quality is still being questioned. Salaries have risen but, in view of the purchasing power of the dollar, the increase has not been as spectacular as the figures would imply. In 1900 the average salary of teachers in cities of over 8000 population was $670; in 1954–55 the estimated average salary of teachers, principals, and supervisors was $3932, equivalent in goods and services to the purchasing power of $2050 in 1935–39. The estimated average salary of elementary-school teachers in 1954–55 was $3614 and of secondary-school teachers was $4194. In a report issued in November 1954, by the Research Division of the N.E.A. it was stated that 11.9 per cent of the

1,066,234 classroom teachers or about 126,880 would receive less than $2500 in 1954–55 in twelve states; in contrast 22.3 per cent or about 237,780 teachers would receive $4500 or more, particularly in those states that have one or more large urban school districts.

Equal salaries must be paid to men and women teachers having the same qualifications in thirteen states, and in most cities a single salary scale has been adopted for elementary and high-school teachers. In thirty-eight states teachers are protected in their tenure after a period of probation, usually of three years. Most of the states authorize the establishment of retirement plans for teachers, generally on a contributing basis; in a few states these plans have been integrated with the federal social-security system since teachers were recently included in it. The employment of married women is permitted generally. Nearly eighty per cent of all the teachers are women, while the better paid administrative positions are held by men.[7]

The preparation, whether in normal schools, teachers colleges, or liberal arts colleges, is not considered to be adequate to turn out finished teachers any more than preparation in any other professional school turns out finished practitioners. The more advanced school systems usually require a period of probation before final appointment. In this period the young teacher is expected to be assisted by his principal or supervisor, or to follow additional courses that may be locally available. The practice of in-service training of teachers which was provided to supplement and fill in gaps in an inadequate system of preservice training has in fact been continued to improve and raise the standards of the profession and to help teachers to keep abreast of the latest developments in educational theory and practice or to advance their mastery of their special subject. The in-service courses may be offered by the local or state authorities or more usually by university departments of education in the form of courses,

workshops, or discussion groups. The most popular of all
forms is the summer school attended annually by an increasing number of teachers. The popularity of in-service courses
may be due to requirements for promotion or increase in
salaries, or standards of accrediting agencies, all described by
the late Professor Edgar W. Knight as "improvement by
degrees." Others claims that in-service education is an urgent
necessity because "new knowledge is being made available
all the time" and teachers must keep abreast of it.

PROFESSIONAL ORGANIZATIONS

Much of the credit for the improvement of the status of
teachers is due to the National Education Association,
founded in 1857 as the National Teachers Association and
established with headquarters in Washington, D.C. The
Association had a membership in 1954 of 561,708, about half
the total number of men and women engaged in the manifold
activities of education — administration, supervision, and
teaching at all levels from the primary to higher education.
The organization has numerous standing committees and
commissions, and some twenty-seven departments affiliated
with it, such as the American Association of School Administrators, the National Association of Elementary School
Principals, the National Association of Secondary School
Principals, the National Council for the Social Studies, and
the Association for Supervision and Curriculum Development, and many others representing the interests of subject-
matter teachers. In the early years of the present century
the Association devoted its attention to the improvement of
the status of teachers; but soon it turned its efforts instead
to raising professional standards and the improvement of
education, a policy which proved more effective in the long
run in securing better working conditions, raising salaries,
providing retirement allowances, and the enactment of tenure
laws. Since 1921 the Association has published a monthly

journal, and since 1922 has maintained a Research Division. In 1935, the N.E.A. and the American Association of School Administrators organized the Educational Policies Commission which has published a series of significant reports, including *The Unique Function of Education in American Democracy* (1937), *The Structure and Administration of Education in American Democracy* (1938), *The Purposes of Education in American Democracy* (1938), *Education and Economic Well-Being in American Democracy* (1940), *The Education of Free Men in American Democracy* (1941), *The Education of* ALL *American Youth* (1944 and 1952), and *The Education of* ALL *American Children* (1948). One of the most active of the N.E.A.'s agencies since the end of World War II has been the Commission for the Defense of Democracy through Education which looked into educational crises under attack and exposed the influences responsible for it. It has only the power of arousing public opinion in the defense of democratic action.

With the N.E.A. are affiliated the state associations which are found in every state and which have organizations of their own, publish journals, and promote the interests of education and of teachers. They have a larger total membership than the N.E.A. There are in addition about 4,000 local teachers associations of which some 2,500 are affiliated with the N.E.A.

The N.E.A., which attempts to advance the cause of education and of teachers, stands for professional group action; it is opposed to such use of strikes as was laid down by the Executive Committee in 1947 in the statement, "The Professional Way to Meet the Educational Crisis." A small percentage of the teachers have chosen the method of striking and have joined either the American Federation of Teachers which is affiliated with the American Federation of Labor, or the Union of Professional Workers of the Congress of Industrial Workers.[8]

SHORTAGE OF TEACHERS AND ITS CAUSES

An account of the status of teachers would today be incomplete, however, if the current and prospective shortage of teachers, which is creating a serious situation for the public schools, were not discussed. The shortage is due not only to the rapid increase in school enrollments, which promises to continue for at least another decade, but also to a number of other causes and more particularly to the demand and opportunity for manpower which arose during World War II and continued almost unbroken in the postwar period. At present, schools and classrooms are overcrowded and children, estimated at 700,000, are being deprived of their full-time schooling. The most serious aspect of the growing shortage of teachers during and since World War II is the lowering of standards for employment of young people on "emergency" or substandard licenses granted after a few weeks or months of training of candidates well-educated otherwise but without any professional preparation. During the war it is estimated that some 300,000 teachers left the profession for better-paid occupations. The supply of teachers has not kept up with the demand and the institutions for the preparation of teachers are graduating only about one-fourth the number of new teachers needed each year. It is this condition that is leading to employment of persons on substandard licenses, particularly in the elementary schools, the available supply of high-school teachers has begun to exceed the demand and some have found employment in elementary schools. The number of teachers on substandard licenses declined from 90,000 in 1950 to approximately 80,000 in 1954–55. In the latter year, the enrollment in all public schools — elementary and secondary — showed an estimated increase of 1,263,000 pupils over the previous year requiring an increase of 43,000 in instructional staff (classroom teachers, principals, and supervisors).[9]

The issue raised by this situation is not wholly one of salaries, although they do constitute an important factor. In an era of prosperity, young people are likely to seek careers that are more remunerative and to disregard the security of the teaching profession. The exodus of teachers has led to a consideration of other influences that may be affecting the teaching profession. Salaries alone are not the determining factors. The task of the classroom teachers has been constantly expanding since the beginning of the century. Both in the elementary and secondary schools the problems of discipline have become more serious. For the emergence of these problems the emphasis on freedom for the child is not the only cause, nor, except in the postwar years, has the increased size of classes produced the disciplinary problems. Those who charge the schools with the responsibility for the rise in juvenile delinquency and expect the school to play the most important part in checking it tend to forget that there is general unsettlement resulting from the shifting of population, changes in the character of the family, a gradual decline in the influence of the home and other social agencies including the church, and the compulsory attendance of many boys and girls who are misfits in the high schools. To all these influences should be added the crises through which the country has passed since 1914 which were contributory to the social changes only partially listed here. The school alone is unable to handle the problems and, while many teachers become discouraged with the disciplinary situations and leave the profession, society itself is only gradually awakening to an understanding of juvenile delinquency and its causes.

But even if teachers were not confronted, especially in the high schools, with these problems their duties have been accumulating. In addition to the functions they are expected to perform in the definition cited on p. 3, they have been found to have increased to such an extent that in order to conserve teacher manpower and to make the most of the abilities of competent teachers it has been proposed that a teacher-aide experiment started in Bay City, Michigan, be adopted elsewhere. With the help of aides it was found in this experiment that teachers spent less time on the following tasks — correcting papers, written lessons, pupil control, taking roll, making reports, transition, and out-of-school tasks. They had more time for lesson plans, group planning, counseling, dictation, reading-to-group, recitation, and free time. It was reported that "elementary classes numbering 45 to 52, with a teacher plus an aide, have made greater progress than classes of 30 under an equally good teacher with no aide." Somewhat similar experiments have been tried elsewhere and recall those tried out at the beginning of the century (see p. 137). These experiments may help in the current emergency arising out of the shortage of teachers, but a certain scepticism may be expressed about its value as a permanent solution.

There are other causes besides salaries and size of classes that may be responsible for the exodus of teachers from the profession. The relations between the administrative officials and classroom teachers are not everywhere as satisfactory as the improved standards of professional preparation warrant. Teachers feel that they are not consulted on matters within their area of competence and that they are not treated as colleagues professionally. Innovations are introduced without the advice of those who are expected to carry them out in the classroom. This is an unfortunate feature of a profession in which there remain too many practices developed at a time when the training of teachers was inadequate. Able and competent teachers, devoted to their work — and the percentage of these is as high as in any other profession — if they do not enter other occupations, are faced with the fact that to gain recognition and more salary and prestige the line of promotion is to enter the ranks of the administrators as principals, supervisors, or superintendents. No system has yet been developed to reward the distinguished classroom teacher. Nor, unfortunately, has any system been discovered to differentiate between the competent and incompetent, although merit and rating scales have been tried out frequently and in many school systems during the past fifty years. Advancements in salary have generally been automatic and increments have been given for further study.

Another reason for the dissatisfaction of teachers with their status is that there are more restrictions on the private lives of teachers than on other members of their community.[10] Such restrictions may extend to the use of alcoholic liquor in public or even in private or to smoking. Social relations between teachers of opposite sexes may be looked upon with suspicion. More rigorous standards may prevail on dress. And teachers are in some communities expected to be more regular than others in church attendance and church activities, including teaching in Sunday school. While such restrictions are gradually being reduced, another form of supervision has had a more deleterious influence on the morale of teachers.

In the postwar hysteria everything that appears to be an innovation in classroom instruction is open to suspicion and teachers who claim the right to teach controversial subjects or to mention Communism are charged with being engaged in subversive activities. Part of the same campaign is an increase in the requirement that teachers sign loyalty oaths, a practice which is not altogether new but which is resented because the oaths are required of the teaching profession alone. Textbooks have been attacked, censored, and rejected on account of some sentences quoted out of context as examples of subversion. The teaching *about* Communism to strengthen the pupils' understanding and appreciation of the ideal of democracy and comprehension of what they read in newspapers, magazines, or books is frowned upon as disloyal. To give pupils some understanding of the United Nations and of Unesco, in both of which the United States is an active member, or any attempt to develop an understanding of the international problem in which the nation is involved may be declared un-American by self-constituted patrioteers and eliminated from the school program because such instruction is considered to be propaganda for a supergovernment to override national sovereignty.

Such restrictions on the private life of teachers and interference with the right to academic freedom which they claim has only helped to aggravate a situation already confused and muddled by the attacks on the public schools for neglecting the fundamentals and fostering "progressive" methods and content of instruction. By the middle of the twentieth century there was ample evidence that fear was spreading among teachers in many areas — fear of being suspected because of their associations, or the books they read, or instruction given in the classroom. This fear was heightened by laws like the Feinberg Law enacted in New York State in 1949 requiring annual reports from every board of education in the state on subversive activities of teachers and by the action of the board of education of New York City compelling them to inform on others suspected of Communism. The morale of teachers in Los Angeles was shaken by the attack on an excellent course of study on Unesco, which was banned. The statistics of the number of members of the teaching profession dismissed from service for disloyalty or subversive or un-American activities during the postwar period have never been collected, but the number would only confirm the view that there has never been any cause for the alarm which was created and whose chief result has been to undermine the morale of teachers and perhaps to desiccate instruction. The activities of fundamentalists in several Southern states in the twenties to prohibit the teaching of evolution could be laughed out of court with ridicule, but the attacks on the schools that accompanied the postwar hysteria could not be ridiculed lest even ridicule might be open to the charge of subversive activity.

The following paragraphs adapted from an editorial by

the author which appeared in *School and Society* in 1948 may be cited as a summary of the present chapter:

It is a paradox in American history that, while faith in education and in the provision of equality of educational opportunity is one of the most deep-rooted of American sentiments, the public esteem of teachers has never paralleled its faith in education. The American public has been trained to spend money on buildings and equipment, but has not yet discovered that its expenditure for teachers is not commensurate with the work expected of them.

In all discussions of measures to put the idea of equality of educational opportunity into effect, the one, and the chief, factor that would implement it has on the whole not been given the attention that it deserves. Buildings are important; equipment is important; and so are textbooks and materials of instruction. But these only provide the conditions under which the educational process can be carried on. Without well-prepared and well-qualified teachers none of these conditions has any meaning. . . .

To provide ready access to schools, colleges, and universities does not in itself guarantee equality of educational opportunity. The only guarantee lies in the teacher. This has been recognized in all proposals for the reconstruction of education wherever they have been put forward not only in the United States but in other countries. The crucial problem everywhere lies in the recruitment, preparation, and remuneration of teachers.[11]

The concluding paragraph of the report mentioned earlier, by Messrs. Jones, Keppel, and Ulich may be added also: "Even the most well-intended universities will be greatly hindered in their endeavors [to widen the base of education] unless they are supported by a change of public opinion. Paradoxically enough, exactly in the American democracy with its loud talk about the value of education, the social role of the educator is not attractive, and the devotion necessary for being a good classroom teacher is inadequately rewarded. Here is a field where the great scholarly associations together with the respected colleges and universities could do inestimable service to the future of the American school." [12]

CHAPTER VI

Education: The Nation's Unfinished Business

The first fifty years of the twentieth century witnessed, for the first time in the history of education, the development and the creation of a school system which is based on the faith of the public in education and which seeks to implement the ideal of equality of educational opportunity for all. Quantitatively, the United States has in the past fifty years set an example to the rest of the world both in the number of children, youth, and adults enrolled in the country's educational institutions and in the amount of money devoted to education. This has been the result not only of the ideal which was set up for the nation when the Republic was established, but also of the belief that education is an investment in human beings. A third reason for the progress made in education has been the recognition of the need of measures to assimilate the large number of immigrants to the American way of life. And a fourth reason has been a growing public consciousness which became more profound during and since World War I that the schools offer the surest safeguards for the preservation of the ideals of democracy in a world in which its existence is threatened by totalitarian ideologies. And at the heart of the American concept of the democratic ideal is a recognition of the worth and dignity of the individual, the realization of which can be promoted by the provision of educational opportunities. There still survives in the background of the American mind the eighteenth-century notion of man's perfectibility or improvability.

There has gradually emerged in the past half century a distinctively American system of education inspired by the traditional faith in education and a desire to implement more successfully the ideal of equality of educational opportunity. This has taken place despite the absence of a central administrative authority such as is found in most other countries to prescribe the aims, organization, and standards of education. The development has been made possible by a large number of factors — the mobility of the people, their desire for a good education for their children, the mobility of teachers, the nationwide use of the same textbooks for the same subjects, the common scheme of school organization, the national professional associations and journals for the discussion of the nation's educational problems, educational publicity, the employment of the same objective tests of intelligence and achievement, and the commonly accepted aim of education for democracy. All these have been forces in the development of a national system of education which reflects the will of the public. The ideals that have inspired this development have been more nearly attained than at any time in the history of education, if judged by the number of children and youth enrolled in the schools, by the amount of money devoted to educational purposes, and the trend to create larger areas of administration to provide richer educational opportunities.

In education, as in many other areas, the first half of the twentieth century has been devoted to adaptation and adjustment rendered necessary by the great social and economic changes that have taken place, by the growth of national sentiment, and later by the recognition of the part to be played by the nation in international affairs. Many influences in the field of education itself stimulated a period of experimentation which characterizes and explains the many changes that took place during the half century. Among the influences that have produced the changes since 1900 were the child-study movement and the development of educational psychology which contributed to a better understanding of the rhythm of the growth of the child and his interests, sounder principles of the learning process, an emphasis on the importance of individual differences in abilities and aptitudes, and the introduction of objective measures of intelligence and achievement. These contributions would of themselves have produced marked changes in school practice, but the changes were hastened by the theories of education that were successively adopted — first Herbartianism and later pragmatism and instrumentalism. The former exercised a profound influence on methods of instruction and the organization of subject matter; the latter stressed activity and growth of the child as the center of the educative process and was deliberately somewhat vague about the curriculum and social aims. Elementary education was more directly influenced by these movements than was secondary education. The character of secondary education changed considerably during the half century but the changes were produced more by the rapid increase in enrollments than by any clearly stated philosophy, and by the entrance into the high schools of large numbers of pupils for whom the traditional academic curriculum was unsuited. The only principle that seems to have governed the changes at this level of education was the desire to give every boy and girl a chance and to discover some educational pabulum that the majority of pupils could digest.

However spectacular the progress of education may have been quantitatively in the past fifty years, the progress has been uneven. Evidence of this was brought to light in the two World Wars by the educational records of the draftees for the nation's armed forces and again by the census of 1940 when information was collected on the education of the population (see pp. 7, 120). The uneven distribution was due

in the main to differences in the distribution of population
and of the wealth that could be taxed for educational purposes. To this might be added the maintenance in the Southern
states of two systems of schools to segregate White and
Negro children. These facts affected every aspect of education — the preparation and salaries of teachers, the buildings
and equipment, and the amount of the expenditures.

Although quantitative criteria can tell only part of a story,
the development of American education quantitatively is a
notable achievement which deserves a tribute. The progress
in the past fifty years has been so rapid and on such a large
scale, and the aims and objectives of education have been
modified so frequently on the plea that it must be adapted to
cultural changes to avoid what was called a cultural lag, that
the attention education demanded was not devoted to quality
of achievement. On the one hand, teachers have been bewil-
dered and confused by the frequent changes in theory and
have taken refuge in routine practices, and, on the other, the
misuse of objective measures led to what Dewey once described as "mechanization, standardization, and quantifica-
tion."

The criticisms of the achievement of students which attracted so much attention after World War II were, indeed,
not new; they recurred frequently. Questions have always
been raised about the low standards obtaining in the area of
fundamentals; and the high schools have admittedly had to
cope with pupils with fourth-, fifth-, and sixth-grade ability
in reading and arithmetic, while the colleges have had to deal
with students inadequately prepared to meet the requirements
of higher education, including ability to read.

These criticisms have been countered by statements that
the teaching of fundamentals, facts, and information — "mere
knowledge" in fact — is not neglected but is subsidiary to the
development of initiative, independence, and originality.
Despite the claims that achievement in fundamentals is as

good or better than in past generations, a best seller, more sensational than factually accurate, attracted public attention in 1955 by its title, *Why Johnny Can't Read*. Greater emphasis has been placed on "know how" than on "know what," on teaching pupils "how to think" rather than "what to think," as though the two are separable. A contempt for intellectualism, which is not new in the American tradition, was strengthened by the interpretation given to Dewey's philosophy.

Another explanation of the inadequate standards of quality attained may be found in the interpretation of the concept of equality in education. Reduced to a narrow equalitarianism, efforts were made to maintain the same standards for all, despite everything that has been written and learned about individual differences of capacity. The result, anticipated more than a century ago by Tocqueville, was the cult of mediocrity. Underlying this trend to mediocrity has been the notion that to differentiate between pupils of different intellectual ability would be undemocratic. The idea of educating an élite was also rejected as undemocratic and some of the traditional subjects in secondary education were even considered to be "aristocratic." One consequence both of this attitude, which rejected the Jeffersonian principle, and of the rapid increase in secondary-school enrollment and the wider distribution of abilities and aptitudes was that the so-called "hard" subjects — languages, mathematics, and science — began to be neglected. The effects of this trend were not realized until World War II, when it was found difficult to secure specialists for the Armed Forces, and after the war when the nation's scientific and technological requirements could not be met because of the inadequate preparation of high-school graduates and when it appeared that the balance between the humanities, natural sciences, and social sciences could only be maintained with difficulty.

These were the reasons for a campaign started after World

War II to discover and train young people of talent. The nation was made aware of the fact that despite all the efforts that had been made to equalize the opportunities for education, large numbers of able boys and girls were unable to continue their education on graduating from the high schools for economic reasons. This situation became a matter of serious consideration at the beginning of the second half of the century and the "education of the gifted" became an important issue, which was met by the creation of scholarship systems by private organizations. The issue also became one of the major subjects of research.

The spectacular development of research in the sciences and the assumed magic of the scientific method stimulated research into every kind of problem in education. The extent of this research can be gauged by turning the pages of Monroe's *Encyclopedia of Educational Research.* Too often research was engaged in for its own sake without any perceptible effect on the practices of the classroom; occasionally some results could be translated into instructional and organizational practice. On the whole, however, the busy occupation with research in education meant a type of restlessness which assumed that the results of instruction were the same as the results of education. Inspired by a certain faith in the miracles of statistical research, the measurement of details was confused with evaluation of the whole process. Schools and pupils were placed under microscopes to watch them grow; the results, if adverse, could be dismissed as unfounded, as they were when it was revealed in several studies that prospective teachers ranked lower than most other students in scholarship and educational equipment.

Despite the great volume of educational literature and discussions of educational problems that has been accumulated in the past fifty years, when the second half of the century opened uncertainty was the prevailing note. The uncertainty as to aims, the rapid expansion of educational facilities, the unexpected rise in the birth rate after World War II, and the serious financial needs — all these are the conditions after half a century that explain the convening of the President's Conference on Education in November 1955. The purpose of the Conference, to which every state sent lay and professional representatives, was to consider problems in education, which seem to have been threshed over many times during the past fifty years without apparently yielding successful answers.

The most crucial problems for the consideration of the Conference were concerned with the financing of education and the recruitment and supply of teachers. The first of these problems arose from the necessity of providing the buildings, classrooms, and equipment to accommodate the largest school enrollment which the country has ever had, and which will pass from the elementary to the high schools in the next decade. There was also involved in this issue the provision of adequate funds for current expenditures, an issue which involves the question of federal aid, and the terms on which such aid may be granted.

The second problem — the staffing of schools — was only in part the result of the increase in the school enrollments. A much larger number of teachers was needed not only because of this increase but also to make up for the exodus of teachers from the profession during and after World War II and the employment in this period of teachers on substandard qualifications. From one point of view the two problems — buildings and staffing — are one, for the recruitment and supply of teachers is as much a financial problem as is the provision of buildings. Something more was involved than finances, however, and this was to organize more successfully than had been done in the past half century the professional preparation and status of teachers, to solve the important issue of securing well-educated men and women who show promise of professional competence in the classroom, and to assay the measures needed to keep such persons in the profession.

After all, it is upon the teachers in the classroom more than upon management and administration that the improvement of the quality of education depends. It is upon the teachers that the responsibility falls for providing an answer to the first question on the agenda of the President's Conference on Education "What should our schools accomplish?" If the history of American education in the past fifty years points to anything it is to the improvement of the qualification of teachers and their status and to the importance of devoting far more attention to the quality of education. It is upon the teachers that the responsibility ultimately devolves of carrying out the aims of education, which still remain to be defined as is evident from the agenda of the conference, the recent unrest among the public, and the criticisms within the profession.

Notes

Chapter I

American Education at Mid-Century

1. The author has developed this thesis in "The Strife of Tongues," the first essay in his *Conflicting Theories of Education* (New York: The Macmillan Co., 1938).

2. See references to Chapter IV, note 14.

3. *A Look Ahead in Secondary Education*, Bulletin, 1951, No. 4 (reprint, 1953), U. S. Office of Education (Washington D.C.), p. 76.

4. The Administration's bill to aid in the construction of buildings, laid before Congress in 1955, represented an attempt to avoid the appearance of control.

5. Boyd H. Bode, "The New Education Ten Years After," *The New Republic*, June 4, 1930, p. 61; John Dewey, "How Much Freedom in New Schools," *The New Republic*, July 9, 1930, pp. 204ff.

6. See Chapter IV, p. 156. On criticisms of education see Vivian T. Thayer, *Public Education and Its Critics* (New York: The Macmillan Company, 1954).

7. See I. L. Kandel, *The Impact of the War upon American Education* (Chapel Hill: University of North Carolina Press, 1948); Eli Ginzburg and Douglas Bray, *The Uneducated* (New York: Columbia University Press, 1953), chapter iv.

8. American Association of School Administrators, *Public Relations for American Schools*, Twenty-eighth Yearbook (Washington, D.C., 1950), p. 27.

9. *National Association of Manufacturers, This We Believe About Education: A Statement Concerning American Education* (New York, 1954), p. 4.

10. Arthur E. Bestor, *Educational Wastelands* (Urbana: University of Illinois Press, 1953), pp. 198 and 208. See also *American Historical Review*, April 1953, pp. 759ff and 777.

11. American Association of School Administrators, *The Ameri-*

can School Superintendency, Thirtieth Yearbook (Washington, D.C., 1952), p. 251.

12. American Association of School Administrators, *Schools for a New World*, Twenty-fifth Yearbook (Washington, D.C., 1947), p. 251.

13. *General Education in a Free Society*, report of the Harvard Committee (Cambridge: Harvard University Press, 1945), p. 43.

14. C. W. Bardeen, "The Man Milliner in Education," *Educational Review*, 57:5ff (January 1919).

15. Nolan C. Kearney, *Elementary School Objectives* (New York: Russell Sage Foundation, 1953), p. 154.

16. *The American School Superintendency*, p. 19.

Chapter II

The Public and Its Schools

1. James Bryce, *The American Commonwealth*, abridged edition (New York: The Macmillan Company, 1905), p. 414.

2. *Circular*, No. 218, September 1952, U. S. Office of Education (Washington, D.C.).

3. Ellwood P. Cubberley, *Public Education in the United States* (Boston, 1919), p. 481.

4. *Statistics of State School Systems 1949-50*, U. S. Office of Education (Washington, D.C., 1952), p. 26.

5. American Association of School Administrators, *The American School Superintendency*, Thirtieth Yearbook (Washington, D.C., 1952), p. 78.

6. N.E.A. Educational Policies Commission, *The Structure and Administration of Education in American Democracy* (Washington, D.C., 1938), p. 78.

7. National Council of Chief State School Officers, *Our System of Schools: A Statement of Some Desirable Policies, Programs, and Administrative Relationships in Education* (Washington, D.C., 1950), p. 6.

8. *The Structure and Administration of Education in American Democracy*, p. 79.

9. Ellwood P. Cubberley in *Encyclopedia of Education*, edited by Paul Monore (New York: The Macmillan Company, 1913), V, 411.

10. *Our System of Schools*, p. 17. See also *State Boards of Education and Chief State School Officers, Their Status and Legal Powers*, Bulletin, 1950, No. 19, U. S. Office of Education (Washington, D.C.).

11. *State Boards of Education and Chief State School Officers*, p. 113.

12. A. S. Draper, *American Education* (Boston: Houghton Mifflin Co., 1909), pp. 84ff.

13. *The Structure and Administration of Education in American Democracy*, pp. 45 and 46.

14. N.E.A. Educational Policies Commission, *Unique Function of Education in American Democracy* (Washington, D.C., 1937), pp. 105ff.

15. President's Advisory Committee on Education, *The Federal Government and Education* (Washington, D.C., 1938), p. 30.

16. See "Rural Education: Sociological Aspects," in *Encyclopedia of Educational Research*, edited by W. S. Monroe (New York: The Macmillan Co., 1950).

17. N.E.A. Educational Policies Commission, *CCC, The NYA, and the Public Schools* (Washington, D.C., 1944).

18. *The Federal Government and Education* (1945), pp. 30, 31.

19. N.E.A. Educational Policies Commission, *Federal-State Relations in Education* (Washington, D.C., 1945), p. 45.

20. See H. S. Ashmore, *The Negro and the Schools* (Chapel Hill: University of North Carolina Press, 1954); Robert M. Williams and Margaret W. Ryan, editors, *School in Transition* (Chapel Hill: University of North Carolina Press, 1954).

21. See J. W. Wise, *The Springfield Plan* (New York, 1945); Hilda Taba and W. Van Til, editors, *Democratic Human Relations* (Washington, D.C., 1945); S. G. Cole, J. Quillen, and M. J. Wiese, *Intercultural Education* (Stanford, 1946); W. H. Kilpatrick and W. Van Til, editors, *Intercultural Activities in the Making*, John Dewey Society, Seventh Yearbook (New York, 1947).

22. N.E.A. Educational Policies Commission, *The Structure and Administration of Education in American Democracy* (Washington, D.C., 1938), p. 123.

23. James Bryant Conant, *Education and Liberty* (Cambridge: Harvard University Press, 1952), p. 81.

24. N.E.A. Educational Policies Commission, *Moral and Spiritual Values in Education* (Washington, D.C., 1951), pp. 6ff.

Chapter III

Education for the Child

1. Walter Lietzmann, "Unterschiede zwischen amerikanisches und deutsches Schulwesen," *Die Erziehung*, 6:18 (1931).

2. "Report of the Committee of Fifteen," *Educational Review*, 9:24 (March 1895).

3. *Ibid.*, p. 231.

4. Frank M. McMurry, *How to Study and Teaching How to Study* (New York, 1909), p. 283.

5. Department of School Superintendence, Tenth Yearbook (Washington, D.C., 1932), p. 76.

6. John Dewey, *My Pedagogical Creed* (1897; cited from 1929 reprint, Washington, D.C.: Progressive Education Association), p. 9.

7. John Dewey, *Democracy and Education* (New York: The Macmillan Co., 1916), p. 225.

8. *New York Times*, October 10, 1944, p. 32.

9. Dewey, *My Pedagogical Creed*, p. 9.

10. Dewey, *Experience and Education* (New York: The Macmillan Co., 1938), p. 102.

11. Boyd H. Bode, *Progressive Education at the Crossroads* (New York: Newsom, 1938), p. 96.

12. Dewey, "Individuality and Freedom," *Journal of the Barnes Foundation*, 1:1ff (1926); also in *John Dewey's Philosophy*, edited by Joseph Ratner (New York: Modern Library, 1939), pp. 617ff.

13. Dewey, "Science and the Future of Society," in *John Dewey's Philosophy*, pp. 343ff.

14. Dewey, *Democracy and Education*, p. 283.

15. Dewey, *Experience and Education*, p. 116.

16. I. L. Kandel, *The Impact of the War Upon American Education*, chapter iii.

17. *Education for American Life: A New Program for the State of New York* (New York, 1938).

18. John L. Childs, *Ten Theses on Education in American Culture* (Greenwich, Connecticut, 1935).

19. W. H. Kilpatrick, editor, *The Educational Frontier* (Chicago, 1933), pp. 318ff.

20. Dewey, *Education and the Social Order* (New York: League for Industrial Democracy, 1936; reprinted 1949), p. 10.

21. W. H. Kilpatrick, *A Reconstructed Theory of the Education Process* (New York, 1935), p. 22.

22. Dewey, *Education and the Social Order*, pp. 6ff.

23. Educational Policies Commission, *The Purposes of Education in American Democracy* (Washington, D.C., 1938), p. vii.

24. *Ibid.*, pp. 50, 72, 96, 108, adapted.

25. E. G. Olsen, editor, *The Modern Community School* (New York, 1953).

26. Kandel, *The Impact of the War Upon American Education*, chapter iii.

27. Department of Elementary School Principals, *Community Living in the Elementary School*, Twenty-seventh Yearbook (Washington, D.C., 1945), pp. 12ff.

28. Willard S. Elsbree and Harold J. McNally, *Elementary School Administration and Supervision* (New York, 1951), p. 376.

29. Hollis L. Caswell and A. W. Foshay, *Education in the Elementary School* (New York, 1950), p. 190.

30. Elsbree and McNally, *Elementary School Administration and Supervision*, p. 61.

31. American Association of School Administrators, *Schools for a New World*, Twenty-fifth Yearbook (Washington, D.C., 1947), pp. 43ff.

32. N. C. Kearney, *Elementary School Objectives* (New York, 1954), p. 43.

33. *Educating Children in Grades Seven and Eight*, Bulletin, 1954, No. 10, U. S. Office of Education (Washington, D.C., 1954), pp. 10ff.

34. *Guide for Elementary Education in 1953-55, Upper Division* (Salem, Oregon, 1953), p. iv.

35. New York State Department of Education, *The Elementary School Curriculum; An Overview* (Albany, 1954), p. 11.

36. *New Primary Manual* (Cincinnati Public Schools, 1953).

37. Arthur B. Moehlman, *School Administration* (Boston, 1951), p. 283.

38. Elsbree and McNally, *Elementary School Administration and Supervision*, p. 162.

Chapter IV

Education of the Adolescent

1. This seems to be implied in the statement by Drs. John Dewey and John L. Childs that "the liberation of creative activity and elevation of aesthetic taste which would follow the reconstruction of the economic system is moreover an illustration of the position we have taken as to the relation of the individual and the social." See *The Educational Frontier* (University of Chicago Press, 1933), p. 298.

2. More recently to disguise the origin of the idea, the word "decorative" has been used.

3. For a fuller discussion of this period, see A. O. Hansen, *Liberalism and American Education: Education in the Eighteenth Century* (New York: The Macmillan Co., 1926).

4. See Wilfred M. Aiken, *The Story of the Eight-Year Study* (New York: Harper, 1942); Dean Chamberlin, Enid Chamberlin, Neal E. Dronght, and William E. Scott, *Did They Succeed in College* (New York: Harper, 1942).

5. Such evidence can be found in: Thomas H. Briggs, *The Great*

Investment (Cambridge: Harvard University Press, 1934); I. L. Kandel, *The Dilemma of Democracy* (Cambridge: Harvard University Press, 1935); John L. Tildsley, *The Mounting Waste of the American High School* (Cambridge: Harvard University Press, 1936); I. L. Kandel, *The Impact of the War Upon American Education*, previously cited.

6. James B. Conant, *Education in a Divided World* (Cambridge: Harvard University Press, 1948), pp. 64 and 228; N.E.A. Educational Policies Commission, *Education of the Gifted* (Washington, D.C., 1954).

7. See Kandel, *The Impact of the War Upon American Education*, pp. 81ff.

8. N.E.A. Educational Policies Commission, *Education for* ALL *American Youth* (1952), p. 14.

9. *Ibid.*, p. 32.

10. *Ibid.*, p. 45.

11. *Ibid.*, p. 151.

12. *Ibid.*, pp. 136ff.

13. *Ibid.*, p. 233.

14. *Ibid.*, pp. 343ff.

15. *Education for* ALL *American Youth* (1944), pp. 407ff.

16. *Education for* ALL *American Youth* (1952), pp. 376ff.

17. *Vocational Education in the Years Ahead*, Vocational Division Bulletin, No. 234, U. S. Office of Education (Washington, D.C., 1945).

18. This Commission was appointed for a three-year term by the U.S. Commissioner of Education, Dr. John W. Studebaker; a second commission was appointed in 1951.

19. The college entrance requirements or the academic courses were included as part of vocational preparation; they ceased to be considered part of the cultural heritage.

20. National Association of Secondary School Principals, *Bulletin*, vol. 31, no. 145, March 1947.

21. *Bulletin*, 1951, no. 22 (reprint, 1953), U.S. Office of Education (Washington, D.C.,), pp. 12ff.

22. *Ibid.*, p. 92.

23. *A Look Ahead to Secondary Education for Life Adjustment*, Bulletin, 1954, no. 4, U.S. Office of Education (Washington, D.C.), p. 76.

24. *Ibid.*, p. 87.

25. *Ibid.*, p. 11.

26. See H. Alberty, *Reorganizing the High School Curriculum* (New York: The Macmillan Co., 1953), pp. 14ff. and 148ff; *Life Adjustment Education for Every Youth*, Bulletin, 1951, No. 22 (reprint 1953), U.S. Office of Education (Washington, D.C.), pp. 10ff.

See also W. H. Kilpatrick and others, *The Teacher and Society*, John Dewey Society, First Yearbook (New York: Appleton-Century Co., 1937), chapter ii; and a leaflet, *Bright Kids: We Need Them*, distributed in February 1955 by the Regents of the University of the State of New York.

27. "Offerings and Enrollments in High School Subjcts, 1948–50," *Biennial Survey of Education in the United States, 1948–50* (Washington, D.C.: U.S. Office of Education, 1951), chapter 5.

28. *General Education in a Free Society*, Report of the Harvard Committee (Cambridge: Harvard University Press, 1945), p. 9.

29. Conant, *Education in a Divided World*, pp. 64 and 228f.

30. N.E.A. Educational Policies Commission, *Education of the Gifted* (Washington, D.C., 1950), pp. 4, 8, 11.

31. Vannevar Bush, *Science the Endless Frontier: A Report to the President* (Washington, D.C., 1945), pp. 130, 135f.

32. Educational Testing Service, *Annual Report to the Board of Trustees 1953–54* (Princeton, N.J.), p. 15.

33. Conant, *Education in a Divided World*, p. 139.

34. See W. Lloyd Warner, R. J. Havighurst, and M. B. Loeb, *Who Shall be Educated? The Challenge of Unequal Opportunities* (New York, 1944); A. B. Hollinshead, *Elmtown's Youth: The Impact of Social Classes on Adolescents* (New York, 1949); W. Lloyd Warner, editor, *Democracy in Jonesville* (New York, 1949).

Chapter V

The Teaching Profession

1. See National Committee on Teacher Education and Professional Standards and the National Education Association, *Manual on Certification Requirements for School Personnel in the United States* (Washington, D.C., 1953).

2. G. A. Richardson, Hélène Brûlé, and Harold E. Snyder, *The Education of Teachers in England, France and U.S.A.* (Paris: UNESCO, 1953); American Association of Colleges for Teacher Education, *Revised Standards and Policies for Accrediting Colleges for Teacher Education* (Oneonta, New York, 1951), p. 18.

3. See Chapter III; and *The Education of Teachers in England, France and U.S.A.*, pp. 270ff.

4. See Chapter IV.

5. James Bryant Conant, "A Truce Among Educators," *Teachers College Record*, 46:156ff (December 1944).

6. See Marten Ten Hoor, "Scholars and Schoolmasters," *Bulletin*

of the American Association of University Professors (Autumn 1954), pp. 375ff; Howard Mumford Jones, Francis Keppel, and Robert Ulich, "On the Conflict between the 'Liberal Arts' and the Schools of Education," *The ACLS Newsletter*, vol. V, no. 2, pp. 17ff; J. Fletcher Wellemeyer, Jr., "Scholars Look at Education," *ibid.*, pp. 39ff.

7. *The Eductaion of Teachers in England, France and U.S.A.*, pp. 298ff; National Education Association, Research Division, *Advance Sheets of Public and Elementary Secondary Schools for the School Year 1954-55*, and *The 1954 Teacher Supply and Demand Report* (Washington, D.C., 1954).

8. T. D. Martin, "The Profession Looks at Itself," *The Annals of the American Academy of Political and Social Science*, September 1949, pp. 157ff; National Education Association *Handbook*.

9. See I. L. Kandel, *The Impact of the War upon American Education*, pp. 61ff; *Advance Sheets of Public and Elementary Secondary Schools for the School Year 1954-55*.

10. Howard K. Beale, *Are American Teachers Free?* (New York: Scribners, 1936).

11. I. L. Kandel in *School and Society*, 67:308ff (April 24, 1948).

12. Jones, Keppel, and Ulich, "On the Conflict between the 'Liberal Arts' and the Schools of Education," p. 38.

Index